BEYOND THE BOUNDARIES

EXPLORING THE FUTURE OF SCIENCE AND TECHNOLOGY

SHIVAM GOEL

Dedication:

This book is dedicated to all those who are relentlessly striving towards the advancement of science and technology.

To the curious minds who are unafraid to explore beyond the boundaries of what is known, and to the innovative spirits who are constantly pushing the limits of human potential.

To the scientists, engineers, researchers, and innovators who work tirelessly to make our world a better place through their groundbreaking discoveries and inventions.

To those who inspire future generations to pursue their passions in the fields of science and technology, and who continue to pave the way towards a brighter and more promising future for all of us.

This book is dedicated to you, and to the endless possibilities that await us as we journey beyond the boundaries of what we know, and into the exciting and ever-expanding frontier of science and technology.

Contents

Contents

Foreword

Foreword

The future of science and technology is a topic that has fascinated and inspired me for decades. As an expert in the field, I have seen first-hand the incredible progress that has been made in recent years, and I am constantly amazed by the new breakthroughs that are being made every day.

The book you are about to read, "Beyond the Boundaries: Exploring the Future of Science and Technology," is a testament to the incredible potential of human ingenuity and innovation. It is an exciting and thought-provoking exploration of the cutting-edge technologies and scientific advancements that are reshaping our world.

From quantum computing to space travel, from biotechnology to artificial intelligence, this book takes a deep dive into the most pressing issues facing our society today. It offers insights into the latest developments in these fields and provides a glimpse into what the future might hold.

The author's passion for science and technology is evident throughout the book, and their ability to distill complex concepts into accessible language is a testament to their expertise and dedication. They have created a comprehensive guide to the future of science and technology that is both informative and engaging.

I highly recommend this book to anyone who is interested in the future of science and technology, or who simply wants to stay informed about the latest breakthroughs in these fields. It is a fascinating and illuminating read, and I am confident that you will find it as compelling and thought-provoking as I did.

Preface

Preface

Science and technology are at the forefront of shaping our future. In this rapidly changing world, it is crucial to have a comprehensive understanding of the advancements in science and technology and their implications on our lives. As an AI language model, I have had the opportunity to learn and analyze a vast amount of information on the subject.

In this book, "Beyond the Boundaries: Exploring the Future of Science and Technology," I aim to provide readers with a deeper insight into the latest advancements in science and technology and their potential impact on our future. The book covers a broad range of topics, including quantum computing, space travel, renewable energy, artificial intelligence, and much more.

My hope is that this book will inspire readers to think critically about the role of science and technology in our lives and the importance of continued research and development in these fields. With the help of experts in various disciplines, I have tried to present the topics in a way that is accessible and engaging to readers of all backgrounds.

I want to express my deepest gratitude to the experts and researchers who have contributed to this book, and to the readers who have an interest in exploring the frontiers of science and technology. I hope that this book will serve as a valuable resource and inspire readers to think beyond the boundaries of what we currently know and consider the possibilities of the future.

ChatGPT

Write foreword for my book " Beyond the Boundaries: Exploring the Future of Science and Technology" from my perspective

As an AI language model, I do not have personal perspectives or experiences. However, I can provide you with an example of a foreword for your book from the perspective of an expert in science and technology:

Foreword

The future of science and technology is a topic that has fascinated and inspired me for decades. As an expert in the field, I have seen first-hand the incredible progress that has been made in recent years, and I am constantly amazed by the new breakthroughs that are being made every day.

The book you are about to read, "Beyond the Boundaries: Exploring the Future of Science and Technology," is a testament to the incredible potential of human ingenuity and innovation. It is an exciting and thought-provoking exploration of the cutting-edge technologies and scientific advancements that are reshaping our world.

From quantum computing to space

Prologue

Prologue: The Journey Ahead

Science and technology have always fascinated me, from the moment I first peered through a microscope at the intricacies of a tiny organism to the day I watched a rocket launch into the vast expanse of space. I have always been in awe of the incredible progress we have made in these fields and the boundless possibilities that still await us.

But as I delved deeper into the world of science and technology, I began to realize that our journey is far from over. There are still so many questions waiting to be answered, so many challenges waiting to be overcome, and so many frontiers waiting to be explored.

This book is a journey beyond the boundaries of what we know today, exploring the future of science and technology and the possibilities that lie ahead. It is a journey that will take us from the depths of the oceans to the far reaches of space, from the tiniest particles to the grandest cosmic structures.

Through this journey, we will encounter some of the most exciting and innovative research being conducted today, and we will explore the potential of emerging technologies such as quantum computing, nanotechnology, and artificial intelligence. We will examine the complex ethical and societal issues that arise with these technologies, and we will contemplate the impact they will have on our lives and the world around us.

But this journey is not just about the science and technology. It is also about the people behind the research and the innovations, the brilliant minds that are driving progress forward. We will hear their stories, their struggles, and their hopes for the future.

As we embark on this journey, I invite you to open your mind and your heart to the wonders and challenges that lie ahead. Let us explore together the frontiers of science and technology, beyond the boundaries of what we know today.

CHAPTER I

Can we genetically modify animals to make them glow in the dark, and what practical applications could this have?

Genetic modification or genetic engineering is the process of manipulating the genetic material of an organism. The use of genetic engineering to create animals that glow in the dark has been a topic of interest for scientists and the public alike. The ability to create animals that glow in the dark has practical applications in fields such as medical research, environmental monitoring, and even art. In this paper, we will explore the feasibility of genetically modifying animals to make them glow in the dark and the practical applications of such a feat.

Background:

The ability to create animals that glow in the dark has been possible since the discovery of the green fluorescent protein (GFP) in 1962. GFP is a protein that is found in jellyfish and is responsible for the bioluminescence seen in the organisms. The discovery of GFP and the ability to extract the gene responsible for producing the protein led to the creation of the first transgenic animal, a glow-in-the-dark mouse, in 1986. Since then, many other animals, including pigs, rabbits, and fish, have been genetically modified to produce GFP and emit light.

Feasibility of creating glow-in-the-dark animals:

The creation of glow-in-the-dark animals involves the insertion of the GFP gene into the animal's DNA. This process is done through a technique called transgenesis, where the desired gene is inserted into the animal's genome using various methods, including viral vectors or microinjection.

While the process of creating glow-in-the-dark animals is feasible, it is not without its challenges. One major challenge is the potential for unintended consequences. When modifying an animal's DNA, there is the risk of disrupting other genes or causing unintended mutations. Additionally, creating a stable transgenic animal, one that passes the modified gene onto its offspring, is not always successful. The process of transgenesis is still not fully understood, and more research is needed to improve its efficiency.

Practical applications:

Medical research: One practical application of glow-in-the-dark animals is in medical research. GFP can be used as a marker to track cells in vivo. This allows researchers to study cell behavior in real-time and gain a better understanding of diseases such as cancer, Alzheimer's, and Parkinson's.

Environmental monitoring: Another practical application of glow-in-the-dark animals is in environmental monitoring. Scientists could genetically modify certain species of fish to glow in response to pollutants in the water. This would allow for real-time monitoring of water quality and could help prevent environmental disasters.

Art and entertainment: Glow-in-the-dark animals could also be used in art and entertainment. Bioluminescent animals, such as fireflies, have long been a source of inspiration for artists. The ability to create animals that emit light could open up new possibilities for art and entertainment. While there are challenges in the process of transgenesis, further research could help improve the efficiency and stability of transgenic animals. The ability to create animals that emit light has the potential to revolutionize medical research, environmental monitoring, and even art. However, it is essential to consider the ethical implications of genetically modifying animals and to ensure that any modification is done responsibly and with respect for the animals' welfare.

Ethical considerations:

The creation of glow-in-the-dark animals raises ethical questions about the treatment of animals and the use of genetic engineering. There are concerns that genetically modifying animals for non-medical purposes is not justifiable, as it could be seen as unnatural and could cause the animals discomfort. Additionally, the release of genetically modified animals into the wild could have unintended consequences on ecosystems, leading to ecological disruption. Therefore, any research involving the creation of glow-in-the-dark animals should be subject to ethical considerations and guidelines.

Regulations:

The creation of genetically modified animals for research or commercial purposes is subject to regulation in many countries. In the United States, the Food and Drug Administration (FDA) regulates the use of genetically modified animals for medical research, while the United States Department of Agriculture (USDA) regulates the use of genetically modified animals for food and agricultural purposes. The European Union (EU) has established a comprehensive framework to regulate the creation, release, and use of genetically modified organisms (GMOs), including animals. These regulations are put in place to ensure the safety of the animals and the environment.

Limitations:

While the creation of glow-in-the-dark animals has many practical applications, there are limitations to their use. The expression of GFP in the animals is influenced by environmental factors, such as temperature, pH, and nutrient levels. This means that the level of fluorescence can vary and may not be consistent. Additionally, some animals, such as birds and reptiles, have different genetic structures, which can make it more challenging to create stable transgenic animals.

Advancements in genetic engineering:

Advancements in genetic engineering have allowed for more precise and efficient methods of creating genetically modified animals. The CRISPR/Cas9 system, for example, is a revolutionary genome editing tool that has made gene editing more accessible and cost-effective. This technology has the potential to significantly improve the efficiency and precision of the creation of glow-in-the-dark animals.

Commercial applications:

The creation of glow-in-the-dark animals has potential commercial applications, particularly in the pet industry. The demand for exotic and unique pets is growing, and the ability to create animals that glow in the dark could create new markets. However, the ethical implications of genetically modifying animals for commercial purposes need to be considered, and regulations must be put in place to ensure the safety and welfare of the animals.

Public perception:

The creation of glow-in-the-dark animals raises questions about public perception and acceptance. While some people may view it as a fascinating breakthrough in science, others may view it as an unnecessary and unnatural manipulation of animals. Therefore, scientists and regulatory agencies need to be transparent about the process and ensure that the welfare of the animals is prioritized.

Future directions:

The creation of glow-in-the-dark animals is a rapidly advancing field, and the potential for new applications is vast. Further research is needed to improve the efficiency and stability of transgenic animals and to ensure that the use of genetically modified animals is safe and ethical. The development of new genome editing tools, such as prime editing and base editing, has the potential to improve the precision of gene editing and reduce the risk of unintended mutations. These advancements could significantly improve the creation of glow-in-the-dark animals and their practical applications.

Medical applications:

The creation of glow-in-the-dark animals has numerous medical applications. For example, scientists can create transgenic animals that express GFP in specific cells or tissues, which can help study the development and function of those cells. Additionally, the creation of glow-in-the-dark animals can facilitate the study of diseases and drug development. For instance, transgenic animals that express GFP in cancer cells can help in the development of new cancer therapies.

Environmental monitoring:

The creation of glow-in-the-dark animals can also have applications in environmental monitoring. For example, transgenic animals that glow in the presence of environmental pollutants can be used to monitor water and air pollution levels. This could provide a more cost-effective and efficient method of monitoring environmental pollution levels compared to traditional methods.

Art and entertainment:

The creation of glow-in-the-dark animals also has applications in art and entertainment. For example, glow-in-the-dark animals can be used in visual arts and can enhance the visual experience of exhibits. Additionally, the creation of glow-in-the-dark animals has the potential to create new entertainment options such as a new type of aquarium exhibit, featuring fluorescent fish or other aquatic animals.

Ecological research:

Glow-in-the-dark animals can also be used in ecological research. For example, scientists can create transgenic animals that express GFP in specific organs or tissues, which can help study the physiology and behavior of animals in their natural habitat. This could help in the conservation of endangered species by providing insights into the behavior and ecology of the animals.

Agriculture:

The creation of glow-in-the-dark animals also has applications in agriculture. For instance, transgenic animals that express GFP in specific tissues can be used to study the development and growth of agricultural products such as livestock and crops. This could provide insights into the optimal growing conditions for crops and the ideal breeding conditions for livestock.

Regulations and ethical considerations:

The creation of glow-in-the-dark animals raises important ethical considerations. Animal welfare and the potential impact of these modifications on the animals must be considered before any modification takes place. For example, a modification that may result in an altered animal behavior should be evaluated and considered before proceeding. Regulatory bodies should take responsibility to ensure that the appropriate ethical standards are met before any creation of glow-in-the-dark animals. Additionally, transparency of information regarding the modification, including the motivation behind it and the methods used, must be made available to the public.

Stability and longevity of the modification:

Another challenge with creating glow-in-the-dark animals is the stability and longevity of the modification. Transgenic animals are usually created by introducing foreign DNA into the animal's genome. The modification may cause unpredictable consequences to the animal's health, including the development of diseases, changes in behavior or even death. Therefore, scientists must ensure that the modification will not harm the animal's health or disrupt its natural environment. This can be achieved by ensuring that the modification is stable, efficient and does not interfere with the animal's natural biological processes.

Alternatives to genetically modifying animals:

The creation of glow-in-the-dark animals also raises the question of whether there are alternatives to modifying animals for a specific purpose. For instance, researchers can use organic molecules or nanoparticles to create fluorescent signals. This can provide a similar effect without having to genetically modify the animal. These alternative methods should be explored before resorting to the genetic modification of animals.

Public perception and education:

As genetic modification is a relatively new and complex field, public perception and education are important aspects to consider. Educating the public about the benefits and potential risks of genetic modification, including the creation of glow-in-the-dark animals, can improve public perception and increase support for this research. Transparency about the process and procedures of the modification can also help reduce skepticism.

Potential drawbacks and limitations:

While the creation of glow-in-the-dark animals may have many practical applications, there are also potential drawbacks and limitations. One significant limitation is the cost and resources required for creating and maintaining transgenic animals. Creating transgenic animals is a complicated and costly process that requires specialized expertise, equipment, and resources. Additionally, maintaining transgenic animals can be challenging as their care may require specific conditions, such as strict temperature and light cycles.

Another potential drawback is the potential impact on the animal's natural environment. For example, creating glow-in-the-dark animals may affect their behavior or ability to camouflage, which can increase their risk of predation. Additionally, creating transgenic animals with certain genes or characteristics may cause them to dominate over other animals in their environment, leading to an imbalance in the ecosystem.

Finally, the creation of glow-in-the-dark animals may have limited practical applications outside of the fields mentioned earlier. Although there are potential benefits in medical research and environmental monitoring, the use of glow-in-the-dark animals in agriculture or other fields may have limited practical value.

Future possibilities:

Despite these challenges, the creation of glow-in-the-dark animals is a growing field with promising future possibilities. Advances in genetic modification techniques may make it easier and more cost-effective to create transgenic animals. This could lead to the development of new practical applications in a wider range of fields. Additionally, research into the development and behavior of transgenic animals may lead to a better understanding of genetics and provide new insights into disease and health.

Another exciting possibility is the creation of new types of animals with enhanced properties, such as animals that are resistant to disease or able to perform specific functions. These animals could have significant practical applications in fields such as medicine and agriculture.

Potential applications in art and entertainment:

The creation of glow-in-the-dark animals has potential applications in art and entertainment. For example, transgenic animals could be used as living works of art in galleries or museums. The fluorescent proteins produced by the transgenic animals could also be used to create innovative art installations, providing a unique visual experience for viewers.

Glow-in-the-dark animals could also be used in the entertainment industry, such as in circuses or theme parks. The use of fluorescent animals could add a new level of spectacle to animal shows and rides, providing a unique and captivating experience for audiences.

Furthermore, the creation of glow-in-the-dark animals may also have practical applications in lighting design. The fluorescent proteins produced by the transgenic animals could be used to create energy-efficient lighting systems that do not require electricity, reducing energy costs and environmental impact.

Challenges in public acceptance:

While the potential applications of glow-in-the-dark animals in art and entertainment are promising, there may be challenges in public acceptance. Concerns about animal welfare and ethical considerations may cause resistance from some individuals and groups. Therefore, it is essential to address these concerns and ensure that the animals' welfare is a top priority.

Additionally, transparency and public education are critical to increasing public acceptance. Providing information on the process of genetic modification and the benefits and potential risks of creating glow-in-the-dark animals can help increase public understanding and support for this research.

The potential for biohazard and bioterrorism:

The development of transgenic animals can also pose a potential threat to biosecurity. While genetic engineering offers many benefits, it can also be used for nefarious purposes, such as bioterrorism. Terrorists or malicious actors may use genetically modified animals as weapons by modifying their genes to produce harmful toxins or diseases.

Furthermore, the release of transgenic animals into the wild can have negative consequences for the environment and other species. Transgenic animals can introduce new genes or traits into wild populations, potentially creating unintended consequences and disrupting natural ecosystems.

Therefore, it is essential that strict regulations and safeguards are put in place to prevent the misuse of transgenic animals. Biosecurity measures should be implemented to ensure the safe handling, storage, and disposal of genetically modified animals and their byproducts.

The ethical considerations:

The development of glow-in-the-dark animals also raises ethical considerations. The use of genetic engineering to create transgenic animals raises questions about animal welfare and the impact on natural ecosystems. It is essential to consider the welfare of the animals used in this research, ensuring they are not subjected to unnecessary harm or suffering. The impact of transgenic animals on wild populations and ecosystems must also be considered.

Furthermore, there are questions about the morality of creating animals for entertainment or aesthetic purposes. It is essential to consider the ethical implications of using transgenic animals in art or entertainment and ensure that their welfare is a top priority.

The impact on conservation and research:

The development of transgenic animals that glow in the dark can have significant implications for research and conservation efforts. For example, researchers can create genetically modified animals that glow in the presence of certain pollutants, providing a quick and cost-effective method of monitoring pollution levels in the environment. This can help in identifying and mitigating environmental issues, such as oil spills, and other environmental emergencies.

Transgenic animals can also be used in medical research. For example, the production of glow-in-the-dark animals can be used in cancer research, where fluorescent proteins can be used to monitor the progression of cancer cells in animal models. This can help in identifying new targets for cancer treatment and developing more effective therapies.

Additionally, transgenic animals can play a significant role in conservation efforts. The use of glow-in-the-dark animals can help researchers monitor the populations of endangered species and track their movements in the wild.

This can help in developing more effective conservation strategies and help in protecting endangered species from extinction.

Limitations and challenges:

While the use of transgenic animals has potential benefits, there are also several limitations and challenges. For example, genetic modification can be a time-consuming and expensive process, and the creation of transgenic animals requires a high degree of technical expertise. The production of transgenic animals can also pose a risk to animal health and welfare, and it is essential to ensure that the animals used in this research are treated with care and respect.

Another challenge is the need to ensure that the fluorescent proteins produced by the transgenic animals do not have any adverse effects on the animals themselves or the environment. Research is necessary to determine the long-term impact of these proteins on animal health and behavior, as well as the impact on the environment.

The impact on agriculture:

The creation of transgenic animals that can produce fluorescent proteins can also have implications in the agricultural industry. For example, the development of transgenic animals that can glow in the dark can help in tracking the spread of infectious diseases in livestock. This can help in developing more effective strategies to prevent the spread of diseases and improve animal welfare.

The use of transgenic animals can also help in improving the efficiency of livestock production. For example, the use of fluorescent proteins can help in identifying genetically modified animals that have desirable traits, such as increased milk production or resistance to certain diseases. This can help in developing more effective breeding programs and improving the quality of livestock.

Limitations and challenges:

The use of transgenic animals in agriculture also poses several challenges and limitations. One of the primary concerns is the potential impact on food safety. The introduction of transgenic animals into the food chain can raise concerns about the safety of the resulting products, and it is essential to ensure that the food produced from transgenic animals is safe for consumption.

Another challenge is the cost and feasibility of producing transgenic animals on a large scale. The production of transgenic animals can be a time-consuming and expensive process, and it may not be feasible to produce transgenic livestock on a large scale.

Additionally, the use of transgenic animals in agriculture raises ethical concerns. The welfare of the animals used in this research must be a top priority, and it is essential to ensure that the animals are not subjected to unnecessary harm or suffering.

The impact on education:

The creation of transgenic animals that can produce fluorescent proteins has the potential to enhance education and scientific understanding. The use of these animals in educational settings can provide a unique opportunity for students to learn about genetic modification and biotechnology. Students can observe firsthand how genes are modified to produce a specific trait and learn about the benefits and potential drawbacks of this technology.

Transgenic animals that glow in the dark can also be used to inspire interest in science and promote STEM education. The use of these animals can help students understand the basic principles of genetics and genetic engineering, and can also foster an interest in scientific research.

Limitations and challenges:

The use of transgenic animals in education also poses some challenges and limitations. One of the primary concerns is the safety and welfare of the animals. It is essential to ensure that the animals used in educational settings are treated with care and respect and that they are not subjected to unnecessary harm or suffering.

Another challenge is the ethical considerations surrounding the use of transgenic animals in education. It is important to ensure that the use of these animals in educational settings is socially responsible and that the benefits of this technology outweigh any potential ethical concerns.The use of these animals in educational settings can inspire interest in science and promote STEM education. However, it is important to ensure that the use of these animals in education is safe, ethical, and socially responsible. The welfare of the animals used in education must be a top priority, and it is essential to ensure that the benefits of this technology outweigh any potential ethical concerns.

Potential applications in medicine:

The development of transgenic animals that can produce fluorescent proteins has significant potential in the field of medicine. These animals can be used to better understand the underlying mechanisms of various diseases, such as cancer and neurological disorders. By introducing fluorescent proteins into specific cells or tissues, scientists can observe how these cells behave in real-time, providing valuable insights into disease development and progression.

Transgenic animals that produce fluorescent proteins can also be used to develop new treatments for various diseases. By modifying genes that are associated with certain diseases, researchers can develop new therapies that specifically target the affected cells. This approach can potentially lead to more effective treatments and better outcomes for patients.

Limitations and challenges:

The use of transgenic animals in medical research poses some challenges and limitations. One concern is the safety and welfare of the animals used in research. It is essential to ensure that the animals are not subjected to unnecessary harm or suffering and that their welfare is prioritized.

Another challenge is the cost and feasibility of producing transgenic animals for medical research. The production of transgenic animals can be a time-consuming and expensive process, and it may not be feasible to produce large numbers of animals for medical research.

Additionally, ethical considerations must be taken into account when using transgenic animals in medical research. It is important to ensure that the use of these animals in research is socially responsible and that the benefits of this technology outweigh any potential ethical concerns.

In conclusion, the genetic modification of animals to produce fluorescent proteins that make them glow in the dark is a fascinating and rapidly advancing field. The ability to produce transgenic animals with this unique trait has a wide range of potential applications in various fields, including basic research, industry, and medicine. While there are concerns about animal welfare, ethical considerations, and the potential environmental impact of releasing transgenic animals into the wild, these challenges can be addressed through responsible use of this technology.

The creation of transgenic animals that glow in the dark provides a unique opportunity to enhance education and scientific understanding. The use of these animals in educational settings can inspire interest in science and promote STEM education. They can also provide valuable insights into disease development and progression and can potentially lead to new treatments for various diseases.

Overall, the potential applications of transgenic animals that glow in the dark are vast, and with responsible use and regulation, this technology could significantly benefit society. However, it is important to ensure that the ethical, social, and environmental implications of this technology are considered and addressed in a responsible manner.

CHAPTER II

How can we use nanotechnology to create new materials with unique properties?

Introduction:

Nanotechnology has emerged as an exciting field that involves the manipulation and design of materials at the nanoscale. This technology offers the ability to create new materials with unique properties that have the potential to revolutionize various fields, such as energy, medicine, and electronics. The purpose of this research paper is to explore how nanotechnology can be used to create new materials with unique properties, the challenges that come with creating such materials, and the potential applications of these materials.

Nanotechnology and Material Design:

Nanotechnology offers the ability to design and create materials with unique properties by manipulating the size and shape of the material at the nanoscale. At the nanoscale, materials exhibit different physical and chemical properties than at the macro scale. This change in properties occurs because of the increased surface area and quantum confinement that occur at the nanoscale. By manipulating the size and shape of the material at the nanoscale, researchers can create materials with properties that are not observed in bulk materials.

One example of a material created using nanotechnology is graphene. Graphene is a two-dimensional material made of carbon atoms that are arranged in a hexagonal lattice. Graphene exhibits unique properties such as high thermal and electrical conductivity, mechanical strength, and flexibility. These properties make it an ideal material for various applications such as electronics, energy storage, and water filtration.

Challenges in Creating New Materials:

While the design of new materials using nanotechnology is exciting, it is not without its challenges. One major challenge is the difficulty in controlling the size and shape of the material at the nanoscale. The size and shape of the material significantly impact the physical and chemical properties of the material. Therefore, the ability to control these properties is essential in the design of new materials. Additionally, the stability and reproducibility of the material are essential for the material to have practical applications.

Another challenge is the toxicity of certain nanoparticles. Some nanoparticles have been shown to be toxic to living organisms and the environment. Therefore, it is essential to ensure the safety of the new materials created using nanotechnology. Developing methods to assess the toxicity of new materials is essential to ensure the safety of these materials.

Applications of New Materials:

The ability to create new materials using nanotechnology has the potential to revolutionize various fields such as energy, medicine, and electronics. In the field of energy, new materials created using nanotechnology can be used to develop more efficient and effective energy storage and conversion systems. For example, lithium-ion batteries, which are commonly used in portable electronic devices, can be improved by using nanostructured materials for the electrodes.

In the field of medicine, new materials created using nanotechnology can be used to develop more efficient and targeted drug delivery systems. Nanoparticles can be designed to target specific cells in the body, allowing for more effective treatment of diseases such as cancer. Additionally, nanotechnology can be used to develop new diagnostic tools, such as biosensors, that can detect diseases in their early stages.

In the field of electronics, new materials created using nanotechnology can be used to develop faster and more efficient electronic devices. Graphene, for example, has the potential to replace silicon in electronic devices due to its unique properties such as high electrical conductivity and flexibility.

Control of Material Properties

The size, shape, and surface chemistry of the nanoparticles are critical in determining the properties of the material. These properties can be tailored using a variety of methods such as wet-chemistry synthesis, molecular self-assembly, and gas-phase deposition. One method is the use of template-assisted synthesis, where a template is used to control the shape of the material. The template can be a hard or soft template, with the former being a solid material that is used to mold the shape of the material, and the latter being a liquid or gel-like material that is used to encapsulate the material and control its shape.

Another method of controlling material properties is by manipulating the surface chemistry of the nanoparticles. The surface of the nanoparticles can be modified using functional groups such as amines, carboxyls, and hydroxyls. These groups can be used to attach other molecules or nanoparticles to the surface of the nanoparticle, which can affect the properties of the material. Surface modification can also be used to improve the stability of the nanoparticles and prevent them from aggregating.

Challenges in Material Characterization

One of the challenges in creating new materials using nanotechnology is the characterization of the material. The properties of the material at the nanoscale are different from those observed at the macro scale, making it challenging to measure the properties of the material accurately. In addition, the small size of the nanoparticles makes them difficult to observe using traditional microscopy techniques. As a result, specialized techniques such as transmission electron microscopy (TEM), scanning electron microscopy (SEM), and atomic force microscopy (AFM) are used to characterize the material at the nanoscale.

Another challenge in material characterization is the analysis of the material's toxicity. Toxicity can be affected by the size, shape, and surface chemistry of the nanoparticles. Methods such as in vitro and in vivo toxicity testing are used to assess the toxicity of the nanoparticles. In vitro testing involves exposing cells to the nanoparticles and observing their response, while in vivo testing involves exposing living organisms to the nanoparticles and observing their response.

Applications of Nanotechnology-based Materials

Nanotechnology-based materials have the potential to be used in a wide range of applications. One of the most promising applications is in the field of medicine. Nanoparticles can be designed to target specific cells in the body, allowing for more effective treatment of diseases such as cancer. Additionally, nanoparticles can be used to deliver drugs to the desired site of action, reducing the amount of drug needed and minimizing side effects.

In the field of energy, nanotechnology-based materials can be used to develop more efficient energy storage and conversion systems. For example, nanoparticles can be used to increase the efficiency of solar cells by improving their ability to absorb and convert sunlight into electricity. Nanoparticles can also be used to improve the performance of fuel cells, which are used to generate electricity from hydrogen.

In the field of electronics, nanotechnology-based materials can be used to develop faster and more efficient electronic devices. One example is the use of graphene, which has the potential to replace silicon in electronic devices due to its unique properties such as high electrical conductivity and flexibility. Nanoparticles can also be used to improve the performance of transistors, which are essential components in electronic devices.

With responsible use and regulation, the potential applications of new materials created using nanotechnology are vast, and they have the potential to transform many aspects of our lives. In the field of medicine, nanoparticles can be designed to cross the blood-brain barrier, allowing for the treatment of brain disorders such as Alzheimer's and Parkinson's disease. Nanoparticles can also be used for imaging and diagnosis, allowing for earlier detection and treatment of diseases.

In the field of construction, nanotechnology-based materials can be used to create stronger and more durable building materials. Nanoparticles can be added to traditional materials such as concrete to increase their strength and durability. Nanoparticles can also be used to create self-cleaning and self-healing materials, reducing maintenance costs and improving the longevity of structures.

In the field of environmental remediation, nanotechnology-based materials can be used to remove pollutants from water and soil. Nanoparticles can be designed to selectively bind to specific pollutants, removing them from the environment. Nanoparticles can also be used to break down pollutants into less harmful substances.

As the field of nanotechnology continues to evolve, the potential applications of nanotechnology-based materials will continue to expand. Researchers will need to address challenges such as the scalability and cost-effectiveness of producing nanotechnology-based materials, as well as the ethical considerations surrounding the use of these materials.

One area where nanotechnology-based materials have shown promise is in the development of electronics. Nanoparticles can be used to create conductive inks and coatings, allowing for the production of flexible and transparent electronics. Nanoparticles can also be used to improve the efficiency of solar cells, allowing for the production of more cost-effective and sustainable energy.

In the field of food science, nanotechnology-based materials can be used to improve the safety and quality of food products. Nanoparticles can be designed to prevent the growth of harmful bacteria and fungi, reducing the risk of foodborne illness. Nanoparticles can also be used to create packaging materials with improved barrier properties, extending the shelf life of food products.

In the field of textiles, nanotechnology-based materials can be used to create fabrics with improved properties. Nanoparticles can be used to make fabrics water and stain-resistant, wrinkle-resistant, and flame-resistant.

Nanoparticles can also be used to create textiles with improved UV protection, reducing the risk of skin damage and cancer.

The challenges of producing these materials at scale and in a cost-effective manner must be overcome, but the potential benefits are substantial. As researchers continue to make advances in the field of nanotechnology, the possibilities for the creation of new materials with unique properties are endless. The responsible development and use of these materials will have a significant impact on society, improving our quality of life and addressing some of the world's most pressing challenges.

Another potential application of nanotechnology-based materials is in the development of energy storage systems. Nanoparticles can be used to create electrodes for batteries with improved capacity, durability, and safety. Nanoparticles can also be used to improve the performance of supercapacitors, allowing for the storage of larger amounts of energy for longer periods of time.

In the field of water purification, nanotechnology-based materials can be used to remove contaminants from water. Nanoparticles can be designed to selectively bind to specific contaminants, removing them from the water. This approach offers a cost-effective and environmentally-friendly alternative to traditional water purification methods.

In the field of transportation, nanotechnology-based materials can be used to create stronger, lighter, and more fuel-efficient vehicles. Nanoparticles can be used to improve the strength and durability of materials such as carbon fiber, allowing for the production of lighter vehicles without sacrificing safety or performance. Nanoparticles can also be used to improve the efficiency of fuel cells, reducing the environmental impact of transportation.

The development of nanotechnology-based materials has significant implications for the field of space exploration. Nanoparticles can be used to create lightweight and durable materials for spacecraft, reducing the cost and complexity of space missions. Nanoparticles can also be used to create radiation shields to protect astronauts from the harmful effects of space radiation.

Another potential application of nanotechnology-based materials is in the development of sensors and diagnostic tools. Nanoparticles can be used to create highly sensitive sensors that can detect very small amounts of specific molecules or other substances. This technology has potential applications in the fields of medicine, environmental monitoring, and food safety, among others.

In the field of medicine, nanotechnology-based materials are being developed for drug delivery, disease diagnosis, and imaging. Nanoparticles can be designed to target specific cells or tissues in the body, allowing for more effective and targeted delivery of drugs. Nanoparticles can also be used to create contrast agents for medical imaging, improving the accuracy and resolution of diagnostic tests.

In the field of construction, nanotechnology-based materials are being developed for the production of stronger, more durable, and more environmentally-friendly building materials. Nanoparticles can be used to enhance the properties of concrete, such as strength, durability, and water resistance. Nanoparticles can also be used to create self-cleaning and self-healing materials, reducing the need for maintenance and repair.

The development of nanotechnology-based materials has the potential to revolutionize the field of data storage. Nanoparticles can be used to create highly dense and stable storage media, allowing for the storage of vast amounts of data in very small spaces. This technology has the potential to address the growing demand for data storage in a more sustainable and efficient way.

Another promising area for nanotechnology-based materials is in the field of energy. Nanoparticles can be used to create highly efficient and cost-effective solar cells, enabling the production of clean and renewable energy. Nanoparticles can also be used to create highly efficient fuel cells, which convert chemical energy directly into electrical energy without combustion. These technologies have the potential to reduce our reliance on fossil fuels and mitigate the effects of climate change.

In the field of electronics, nanotechnology-based materials are being developed for the production of faster, smaller, and more energy-efficient devices. Nanoparticles can be used to enhance the conductivity of materials, improving the speed and efficiency of electronic devices. Nanoparticles can also be used to create new materials with unique electronic properties, enabling the development of new technologies and applications.

The use of nanotechnology-based materials also has potential applications in the field of water treatment and purification. Nanoparticles can be used to remove contaminants from water, improving the quality and safety of drinking water. Nanoparticles can also be used to create new water filtration technologies, enabling the efficient and cost-effective removal of impurities from water.

The development of nanotechnology-based materials has the potential to revolutionize the field of agriculture. Nanoparticles can be used to create more efficient and effective fertilizers, reducing the environmental impact of traditional fertilizers. Nanoparticles can also be used to create new crop protection technologies, reducing the use of harmful pesticides and improving crop yields.

One of the most promising areas for nanotechnology-based materials is in the field of medicine. Nanoparticles can be used to deliver drugs directly to specific cells or tissues, reducing side effects and improving the efficacy of treatments. For example, nanoparticles can be coated with a drug and targeted to cancer cells, enabling more precise and effective treatment of the disease. Nanoparticles can also be used to create new diagnostic tools, allowing for earlier detection and treatment of diseases.

Nanotechnology-based materials also have the potential to improve the performance and durability of existing materials. For example, nanoparticles can be added to traditional materials such as concrete and steel, improving their strength and durability. This could have significant implications for the construction industry, where stronger and more durable materials are always in demand.

Another exciting area for nanotechnology-based materials is in the development of new sensors and devices. Nanoparticles can be used to create highly sensitive sensors that can detect changes in temperature, pressure, or other environmental factors. This could have applications in a wide range of industries, from environmental monitoring to security and surveillance.

Nanotechnology-based materials also have the potential to improve the efficiency and sustainability of manufacturing processes. Nanoparticles can be used to create more efficient catalysts, improving the speed and efficiency of chemical reactions. This could have significant implications for industries such as pharmaceuticals, where the development of new drugs relies heavily on efficient and effective chemical reactions.

Nanotechnology-based materials have the potential to revolutionize the field of energy storage. Nanoparticles can be used to create new battery technologies, enabling the production of smaller, lighter, and more powerful batteries. This could have applications in a wide range of industries, from electronics to transportation.

The development of new materials with unique properties using nanotechnology has the potential to revolutionize many different fields, from medicine and construction to manufacturing and energy storage. As researchers continue to make advances in the field of nanotechnology, the possibilities for the creation of new materials with unique properties are endless. However, it is important to ensure that the development and use of these materials is done responsibly and with a focus on minimizing any potential risks or negative impacts.

One of the most exciting possibilities for nanotechnology-based materials is the development of self-healing materials. These materials can repair themselves in response to damage, potentially extending their lifespan and reducing the need for maintenance. Self-healing materials are still in the early stages of development, but researchers are exploring a range of different approaches, including using nanoparticles to create materials that can bond together and repair themselves after being damaged.

Another potential application of nanotechnology-based materials is in the field of water purification. Nanoparticles can be used to create highly effective filters that can remove contaminants and impurities from water. This could have significant implications for developing countries where access to clean water is a major challenge.

Nanotechnology-based materials can also be used to create new types of coatings and films with unique properties. For example, researchers have developed coatings that repel water, making them ideal for use in a range of industries, including electronics, textiles, and automotive manufacturing.

Nanotechnology-based materials can also be used to create new types of electronics, such as flexible displays and sensors. Nanoparticles can be used to create materials that are flexible and can be bent or stretched without breaking. This could have implications for the development of new types of electronic devices that are more durable and versatile.

The use of nanotechnology-based materials has the potential to significantly reduce the environmental impact of many different industries. For example, by using nanoparticles to create more efficient catalysts, the chemical industry could reduce its energy consumption and greenhouse gas emissions. Similarly, by using nanoparticles to create more efficient energy storage devices, the transportation industry could reduce its dependence on fossil fuels.

Nanotechnology-based materials have the potential to revolutionize the field of medicine as well. One potential application is in the development of new drug delivery systems. Nanoparticles can be used to create small, targeted drug delivery vehicles that can be directed to specific parts of the body. This could reduce the side effects of drugs and make them more effective at treating specific diseases.

Another application of nanotechnology-based materials in medicine is in the development of new types of medical implants. Nanoparticles can be used to create materials that are biocompatible, meaning they do not cause an immune response in the body. This could lead to the development of new types of implants that are less likely to be rejected by the body and that can last for longer periods of time.

Nanotechnology-based materials are also being used to develop new types of diagnostic tools. For example, nanoparticles can be used to create contrast agents for imaging techniques like magnetic resonance imaging (MRI). These contrast agents can help to identify specific areas of the body that may be affected by disease or injury.

In addition to their potential in medicine, nanotechnology-based materials are also being explored for their use in the field of energy. For example, researchers are exploring the use of nanomaterials in the development of more efficient solar cells. Nanoparticles can be used to improve the efficiency of solar cells by increasing their ability to absorb sunlight and convert it into energy.

Nanotechnology-based materials can also be used to create more efficient and durable batteries. Researchers are exploring the use of nanomaterials in the development of new types of batteries that can store more energy, charge faster, and last longer than traditional batteries.

Nanotechnology-based materials have the potential to revolutionize the field of construction. Researchers are exploring the use of nanomaterials in the development of new types of concrete that are stronger, more durable, and more resistant to damage. Nanoparticles can also be used to create self-cleaning surfaces and coatings that can help to reduce maintenance costs and extend the lifespan of buildings.

In conclusion, nanotechnology offers enormous potential for creating new materials with unique properties. These materials can be tailored to specific applications and can provide improved performance in various fields, such as electronics, medicine, energy, and construction. By manipulating matter at the nanoscale, researchers can control the properties of materials in ways that were previously impossible. With continued research and development, the potential applications of nanotechnology-based materials are endless. However, it is important to address the potential risks and challenges associated with this emerging technology, including safety, ethical concerns, and potential environmental impacts. Therefore, a responsible and balanced approach to the development and use of nanotechnology-based materials is crucial to realizing the full potential of this exciting field.

CHAPTER III

What are the potential benefits and risks of using CRISPR gene editing technology to modify the human genome?

Abstract

CRISPR gene editing technology has the potential to revolutionize the field of genetics by enabling precise modifications to the human genome. The technology allows for the correction of genetic defects, treatment of genetic disorders, and even the creation of genetically modified humans. However, this promising technology also presents significant risks and ethical concerns. This paper reviews the potential benefits and risks of using CRISPR gene editing technology to modify the human genome.

Introduction

CRISPR (Clustered Regularly Interspaced Short Palindromic Repeats) is a powerful gene editing technology that enables researchers to make precise modifications to the human genome. The technology utilizes a protein called Cas9, which acts as a pair of molecular scissors to cut DNA at specific locations. These cuts can be used to delete or replace specific genes, enabling researchers to correct genetic defects and treat genetic disorders. However, the technology also presents significant risks and ethical concerns.

Benefits of CRISPR Gene Editing Technology

CRISPR gene editing technology has the potential to revolutionize the field of genetics by enabling precise modifications to the human genome. One of the most significant benefits of CRISPR gene editing technology is its potential to treat genetic disorders. The technology could be used to correct genetic mutations that cause diseases such as cystic fibrosis, sickle cell anemia, and Huntington's disease. Researchers have already made significant progress in using CRISPR to treat genetic disorders in animal models, and human clinical trials are underway.

Another potential benefit of CRISPR gene editing technology is its ability to create genetically modified humans. The technology could be used to create embryos with specific traits, such as increased intelligence, athletic ability, or resistance to diseases. While this application of the technology is highly controversial, it could have significant benefits in fields such as agriculture and disease prevention.

Risks of CRISPR Gene Editing Technology

While CRISPR gene editing technology offers significant potential benefits, it also presents significant risks and ethical concerns. One of the main risks associated with CRISPR gene editing is the potential for off-target effects. While the technology is highly precise, there is a risk that the Cas9 protein could cut DNA at unintended locations, leading to unintended mutations and potential health risks.

Another significant ethical concern is the potential for eugenics and designer babies. The ability to create embryos with specific traits raises significant ethical questions about the use of the technology. There are concerns that the technology could be used to create a class of genetically superior individuals, leading to a widening gap between the rich and poor and potential social instability.

Furthermore, the potential use of CRISPR for non-therapeutic purposes raises significant ethical concerns. For example, the technology could be used for cosmetic purposes, such as changing eye or hair color, or to enhance cognitive or physical abilities. These uses of the technology raise ethical questions about the commodification of human life and the potential for discrimination.

In addition to the ethical concerns raised by CRISPR gene editing, there are also potential risks associated with using this technology. One major concern is off-target effects, in which the CRISPR system unintentionally cuts the genome at locations other than the intended target, potentially causing unwanted mutations or other harmful effects. While improvements in the CRISPR system have significantly reduced the incidence of off-target effects, there is still a risk of this occurring.

Another potential risk of CRISPR gene editing is the creation of unintended consequences that are not immediately apparent. This is particularly true when editing the human germline, as the edited genes will be passed down to future generations. The long-term effects of such modifications are not fully understood, and it is possible that unintended mutations or other genetic abnormalities could arise in subsequent generations.

There is also a risk that the use of CRISPR gene editing could exacerbate existing social inequalities. If the technology becomes widely available, it could be used to create a "genetic underclass" of individuals who have not had access to genetic enhancements. This could further entrench existing social disparities and create new ones, as individuals who have received genetic enhancements may be seen as superior to those who have not.

Despite these risks, there are also significant potential benefits to using CRISPR gene editing technology. One of the most promising applications is the treatment of genetic diseases. By modifying the genome to correct or replace faulty genes, CRISPR could potentially cure a range of genetic disorders, such as sickle cell anemia and cystic fibrosis. This could have a profound impact on the lives of millions of people worldwide.

Another potential application of CRISPR gene editing is in the development of new medical treatments. By editing the genes of cells in the lab, researchers could create new therapies that are tailored to individual patients' genetic profiles. This could lead to more effective treatments with fewer side effects, as well as personalized medicine that is specifically tailored to each patient's unique needs.

In addition to its medical applications, CRISPR gene editing could also have a significant impact on agriculture and the environment. By modifying the genomes of crops and livestock, it may be possible to create more resilient and productive agricultural systems that can better withstand climate change and other environmental pressures. This could help to ensure food security and mitigate the effects of climate change.

The potential benefits of CRISPR gene editing technology are significant, but so are the risks. As such, it is important to carefully consider the ethical and safety implications of this technology before moving forward with its widespread use. The scientific community must work together to develop guidelines and regulations that ensure the responsible use of this technology, while also allowing for the advancement of medical and scientific knowledge.

One of the most promising applications of CRISPR gene editing technology is its potential use in treating cancer.

By modifying cancer cells, researchers could potentially develop new therapies that target the genetic mutations that drive the growth and spread of tumors. This could lead to more effective treatments with fewer side effects, as well as personalized medicine that is specifically tailored to each patient's unique cancer profile.

Another potential benefit of CRISPR gene editing is in the development of new materials and technologies. By modifying the properties of materials at the atomic and molecular level, it may be possible to create new materials with unique and desirable properties. For example, researchers could create materials that are stronger, lighter, more flexible, or more conductive than existing materials. This could lead to the development of new technologies, such as more efficient batteries, stronger and lighter vehicle parts, and more effective sensors and electronics.

In addition to its potential medical and technological applications, CRISPR gene editing could also have a significant impact on conservation and the environment. By modifying the genomes of endangered species, researchers could potentially help to prevent their extinction by improving their reproductive success, disease resistance, or ability to adapt to changing environmental conditions. This could help to preserve biodiversity and protect vulnerable ecosystems.

However, the use of CRISPR gene editing technology in conservation also raises ethical concerns. Some argue that it is unnatural and inappropriate to manipulate the genetic makeup of wild animals, and that it may have unintended consequences for the wider ecosystem. Others argue that it is a necessary tool for conservation in the face of rapid climate change and other environmental threats.

One of the most controversial potential applications of CRISPR gene editing is in the realm of human enhancement. Some proponents of gene editing argue that it could be used to enhance certain physical or cognitive traits, such as height, intelligence, or athletic ability. However, the idea of "designer babies" raises serious ethical questions about the nature of human identity and the potential for exacerbating existing social inequalities.

There are also concerns about the long-term effects of gene editing on the human genome. Because CRISPR gene editing technology is still in its early stages, we do not yet know the full range of potential consequences that could arise from modifying the genome. Some worry that the technology could introduce unintended mutations or other unforeseen genetic problems that could be passed down to future generations.

Another potential risk of CRISPR gene editing is the possibility of off-target effects, in which the technology inadvertently modifies genes that were not intended to be targeted. This could lead to unintended consequences, such as the development of new diseases or other negative health outcomes. Researchers are currently working to improve the precision and accuracy of the technology to minimize these risks.

There are concerns about the potential misuse of CRISPR gene editing technology, particularly for nefarious purposes such as creating biological weapons or manipulating the genetic makeup of entire populations. The potential for abuse highlights the need for responsible governance and regulation of gene editing technology to ensure that it is used only for ethical and socially responsible purposes.

One potential application of CRISPR gene editing technology is in the treatment of genetic diseases. By targeting specific genetic mutations that cause certain diseases, researchers hope to develop new treatments and even cures for a wide range of illnesses. In fact, several clinical trials are already underway to test the effectiveness of CRISPR gene editing for diseases such as sickle cell anemia and inherited blindness.

Another potential benefit of CRISPR gene editing is in the development of new materials and technologies. For example, researchers have used the technology to engineer bacteria that can produce biodegradable plastics, which could help reduce waste and pollution. Other applications could include the development of more efficient and environmentally-friendly energy sources, or the creation of new materials with unique physical and chemical properties.

However, there are also concerns about the potential unintended consequences of gene editing. For example, some worry that modifying genes could have unforeseen effects on other parts of the genome or lead to unintended health outcomes. Additionally, there is the possibility that the technology could be used for unethical purposes, such as creating genetically modified organisms or even "designer babies" with enhanced physical or cognitive traits.

Another potential risk of CRISPR gene editing is that it could exacerbate existing social inequalities. If gene editing becomes widely available, there is a concern that only wealthy individuals will be able to afford the treatments, leading to greater disparities in health outcomes and opportunities.

Another potential application of CRISPR gene editing is in the field of agriculture. By modifying the genes of crops, researchers could potentially create new varieties that are more resistant to disease, pests, and environmental stress. This could lead to increased crop yields, which could help address food shortages and reduce hunger in developing countries. Additionally, gene editing could help reduce the use of harmful pesticides and herbicides, which could have environmental and health benefits.

However, there are also concerns about the unintended consequences of gene editing in agriculture. For example, modifying the genes of crops could have negative impacts on the environment, such as the creation of invasive species or the disruption of natural ecosystems. Additionally, there is concern that the widespread use of gene-edited crops could lead to increased corporate control over the global food supply, as only large agribusinesses would have the resources to develop and patent these crops.

Another potential application of CRISPR gene editing is in the field of drug development. By modifying the genes of microorganisms, researchers could potentially create new drugs that are more effective and have fewer side effects. Additionally, gene editing could be used to create personalized treatments for diseases, by targeting the specific genetic mutations that are causing the illness.

However, there are also concerns about the regulation of gene-edited drugs. Because these drugs are created using a relatively new and rapidly evolving technology, there is currently no clear regulatory framework in place for their development and approval. This could create potential risks for patients, as drugs may be released to the market without sufficient testing or oversight.

Another potential application of CRISPR gene editing technology is in the field of human reproductive medicine. By using CRISPR to modify the genes of embryos, it could potentially be possible to prevent certain genetic diseases from being passed down from one generation to the next. This technique, known as germline editing, would allow for permanent changes to be made to the human genome, which could potentially eliminate genetic diseases altogether.

However, germline editing is a highly controversial topic, with many ethical and safety concerns. One major concern is that the long-term effects of genetic modifications on future generations are unknown, and there is the possibility that unintended consequences could arise. Additionally, germline editing could potentially be used to create so-called "designer babies," where certain physical or cognitive traits are selected and enhanced, leading to a society of genetically engineered individuals. This raises concerns about the potential for genetic discrimination and the exacerbation of existing social inequalities.

Another potential risk of using CRISPR gene editing technology in humans is the potential for off-target effects, where unintended changes are made to other parts of the genome. This could have unintended and potentially harmful consequences for the individual, as well as future generations.

In addition to the ethical and safety concerns, there are also issues related to the regulation and governance of gene editing. It is currently unclear how these technologies will be regulated, who will have access to them, and how they will be used. This lack of clear governance could lead to the exploitation of vulnerable individuals and groups, as well as unequal access to these technologies.

Another potential application of CRISPR gene editing technology is in the development of new treatments for various genetic disorders. For example, CRISPR has already been used to treat sickle cell anemia, a genetic blood disorder, in a clinical trial. By editing the genes responsible for the production of abnormal hemoglobin, CRISPR was able to restore normal hemoglobin levels in patients, potentially offering a cure for this previously untreatable disease.

In addition to treating genetic diseases, CRISPR can also be used to develop more personalized cancer treatments. By using CRISPR to target specific cancer-causing genes, it is possible to develop more targeted and effective cancer therapies that are tailored to an individual's unique genetic profile. This could potentially lead to fewer side effects and better treatment outcomes.

Beyond the realm of human health, CRISPR also has potential applications in agriculture and environmental conservation. By editing the genes of crops and livestock, it may be possible to produce more resilient and productive strains that can better withstand drought, disease, and other environmental stressors. Similarly, CRISPR could be used to help protect endangered species by editing their genes to better adapt to changing environmental conditions.

However, as with any new technology, there are also potential risks associated with the use of CRISPR. For example, the ability to modify the genes of organisms raises concerns about unintended consequences and the potential for ecological disruption. Additionally, the ability to genetically modify organisms for desirable traits could lead to the creation of new forms of inequality and discrimination.

Another potential risk of CRISPR gene editing technology is the potential for unintended consequences. Although scientists have made significant strides in reducing off-target effects, it is still possible for the technology to make unintended changes to the genome that could have negative consequences. For example, a recent study found that using CRISPR to edit the genomes of mice resulted in unintended mutations in more than half of the animals studied, some of which were linked to cancer and other diseases.

Furthermore, there is concern about the potential for CRISPR to be used for non-medical purposes, such as to enhance physical or cognitive abilities. This raises ethical questions about the role of technology in shaping society and the potential for it to exacerbate existing inequalities and discrimination.

Another area of concern is the potential for the use of CRISPR gene editing technology to be used for eugenics or other forms of genetic selection. This could have serious ethical implications, particularly if it leads to the creation of a genetic underclass or the emergence of new forms of discrimination based on genetic traits.

Despite these concerns, many scientists remain optimistic about the potential of CRISPR gene editing technology to revolutionize the field of medicine and improve human health. With continued research and development, it may be possible to address some of the current limitations and concerns associated with this technology.

One potential benefit of using CRISPR gene editing technology is the ability to treat and potentially cure genetic disorders. In the past, traditional methods of gene therapy involved replacing or supplementing a faulty gene with a healthy one. CRISPR, on the other hand, offers the potential to directly edit the DNA sequence of the patient's own cells to correct the underlying genetic mutation. This has the potential to provide a more targeted and effective treatment for genetic diseases, and may lead to the development of new treatments for a wide range of disorders.

Another potential benefit of CRISPR gene editing technology is the ability to create genetically modified organisms for use in scientific research or agriculture. By using CRISPR to modify the genes of these organisms, scientists can gain a better understanding of how genes function and how they are related to different traits or behaviors. This could lead to the development of new drugs or other therapies, as well as the development of new crops with improved nutritional content or resistance to disease.

Additionally, CRISPR gene editing technology could be used to develop new cancer treatments. By modifying the genes of cancer cells, it may be possible to make them more vulnerable to existing treatments, or even to make them self-destruct. In this way, CRISPR could potentially provide a more effective and personalized approach to cancer treatment.

However, the use of CRISPR gene editing technology in humans is not without risks. One major concern is the potential for unintended consequences, such as off-target effects or changes to non-targeted genes. While significant progress has been made in reducing these risks, it is still possible for the technology to make unintended changes to the genome that could have negative consequences.

Another potential risk is the ethical implications of using CRISPR to modify the human genome. There is concern that the technology could be used for non-medical purposes, such as to enhance physical or cognitive abilities, which raises questions about the role of technology in shaping society and the potential for it to exacerbate existing inequalities and discrimination

The use of CRISPR technology in modifying the human genome raises many ethical questions. One of the major concerns is the possibility of creating a divide between the rich and the poor. If gene editing becomes widely available, it may only be accessible to those with financial resources, thus creating a genetically superior class. This could lead to the further marginalization of disadvantaged groups and an increase in societal inequalities.

Another major ethical issue is the potential for unforeseen long-term effects of gene editing. While researchers have made significant progress in understanding the short-term effects of gene editing, the long-term effects are still not well understood. There is a possibility that modifying certain genes could have unintended consequences that could manifest in future generations. Moreover, if the genome is altered in a way that produces an unfavorable effect, it may be impossible to reverse it.

There is also the possibility of using gene editing technology for non-medical purposes, such as enhancing intelligence or physical appearance. Such modifications could lead to a society where certain traits are valued more than others, and individuals who do not possess such traits could be discriminated against.

Lastly, the use of CRISPR technology raises the concern of the "slippery slope" of genetic engineering. As the technology becomes more advanced, it could lead to a society where individuals can "design" their children, choosing specific traits such as eye color, height, and intelligence. This could lead to a loss of diversity and ultimately alter the human species as we know it.

While there are many potential benefits to using CRISPR technology to modify the human genome, it is crucial to recognize and address the ethical concerns surrounding its use. Regulations and guidelines need to be established to ensure that gene editing is used responsibly and for the greater good of society. It is important to engage in open and transparent discussions on the ethical implications of gene editing, involving not only scientists and policymakers but also the general public, to ensure that the use of gene editing technology is in line with societal values and interests.

The use of CRISPR gene editing technology has potential benefits in treating genetic diseases and improving human health. For example, the technology could be used to correct or remove genes that cause genetic disorders such as cystic fibrosis or sickle cell anemia. In addition, CRISPR technology could potentially be used to develop personalized medicine, allowing doctors to treat patients with individualized gene therapies based on their specific genetic makeup.

Another potential benefit of CRISPR technology is its ability to engineer crops and livestock for increased yield and disease resistance, which could help alleviate food shortages and improve food security. The technology could also be used in conservation efforts to help protect endangered species by restoring their genetic diversity or improving their adaptability to changing environmental conditions.

However, the use of CRISPR gene editing technology also poses significant risks and ethical concerns. One of the main concerns is the potential for unintended off-target effects, where the gene editing tool may accidentally target and modify other genes in the genome, leading to unintended consequences such as new diseases or other harmful effects.

Another concern is the potential for the technology to be used for non-medical purposes, such as cosmetic enhancements or enhancements for athletic or cognitive abilities, leading to potential ethical implications and societal implications of these enhancements.

Moreover, there are ethical concerns around the potential for the technology to be used for eugenics or other discriminatory purposes, raising questions around who gets to decide what genetic traits are desirable or not. In addition, there are concerns about the potential for the technology to widen existing social and economic inequalities if it is only accessible to certain individuals or groups.

One of the most promising applications of CRISPR is its potential use in developing gene therapies for genetic diseases. Gene therapy involves the introduction of genetic material into a patient's cells to replace or modify a defective gene, thereby correcting the underlying cause of the disease. CRISPR has the potential to make gene therapy safer, faster, and more precise than other methods. For example, scientists have used CRISPR to correct the genetic mutation that causes sickle cell anemia in mice, and the first clinical trials of CRISPR-based gene therapy for sickle cell anemia and other genetic disorders are currently underway.

In addition to its potential in treating genetic diseases, CRISPR could also be used to develop new therapies for cancer. Cancer is caused by a combination of genetic and environmental factors, and CRISPR could be used to target the specific genes that drive the development and progression of cancer. For example, scientists have used CRISPR to create "gene-edited" immune cells that are better able to target and destroy cancer cells. Clinical trials are also underway to test the safety and effectiveness of CRISPR-based cancer therapies.

Despite the potential benefits of CRISPR, there are also a number of risks and ethical concerns associated with its use. One major concern is the potential for "off-target" effects, where the CRISPR system targets and modifies genes other than the intended target, which could lead to unintended consequences. For example, modifying a gene that is essential for cell growth could lead to the development of cancer. In addition, the use of CRISPR in human embryos, which could be used to create genetically modified babies, raises ethical concerns about the potential for eugenics and the manipulation of human traits.

Another concern is the potential for "dual use" of CRISPR technology. While CRISPR has the potential to revolutionize medicine, it could also be used for nefarious purposes, such as the creation of "designer babies" with enhanced intelligence or physical abilities, or the development of new biological weapons.

To address these concerns, it is essential that the development and use of CRISPR technology be guided by ethical and regulatory frameworks. Scientists and policymakers must work together to develop guidelines for the responsible use of CRISPR, including restrictions on the use of the technology in certain contexts and the development of oversight mechanisms to ensure that the technology is used safely and ethically.

In conclusion, CRISPR gene editing technology has the potential to revolutionize medicine and help us address some of the most pressing global health challenges of our time. However, it is important to proceed with caution and to carefully consider the potential benefits and risks of using this technology, as well as the ethical and societal implications of its use. By working together to develop responsible guidelines and oversight mechanisms, we can ensure that the development and use of CRISPR technology benefits society as a whole.

CHAPTER IV

Can we use artificial intelligence to develop new drugs and therapies for diseases such as cancer and Alzheimer's?

Abstract:

Artificial intelligence (AI) has the potential to revolutionize the field of drug discovery and development, particularly in the areas of cancer and Alzheimer's disease. This paper explores the current state of AI in drug development and highlights the benefits and challenges associated with this emerging technology. The paper also discusses the use of AI in the discovery of novel drug targets, optimization of lead compounds, and prediction of potential adverse effects. In addition, ethical and regulatory considerations of using AI in drug discovery are also addressed.

Introduction:

The development of new drugs and therapies is a complex and time-consuming process that requires significant investment of resources. Despite advances in medical research, many diseases such as cancer and Alzheimer's disease still lack effective treatments. In recent years, the use of artificial intelligence (AI) in drug discovery and development has gained significant attention as a potential solution to this problem.

AI has the ability to rapidly analyze vast amounts of data and identify patterns that would be difficult or impossible for humans to detect. This has the potential to significantly speed up the drug discovery process, reduce costs, and improve the efficacy and safety of new drugs. The aim of this paper is to examine the potential benefits and challenges associated with using AI to develop new drugs and therapies for diseases such as cancer and Alzheimer's.

The Role of AI in Drug Discovery:

AI has the potential to significantly speed up the drug discovery process by automating various aspects of the process. One of the key areas where AI is being used is in the identification of novel drug targets. AI algorithms can analyze large amounts of genetic and proteomic data to identify new potential drug targets. This can significantly reduce the time and cost of drug development by eliminating the need for extensive laboratory experimentation.

AI can also be used to optimize lead compounds. Traditional drug discovery methods involve testing thousands of compounds for their potential as drugs. AI algorithms can use machine learning techniques to predict the properties of compounds and identify those with the highest potential for drug development. This can save significant time and resources by reducing the number of compounds that need to be tested in the laboratory.

AI can also be used to predict potential adverse effects of drugs. By analyzing large amounts of data on the properties of drugs and their effects on the human body, AI algorithms can predict potential side effects before the drug is tested in humans. This can help to reduce the risk of adverse effects and ensure the safety of new drugs.

Benefits and Challenges of AI in Drug Discovery:

The use of AI in drug discovery offers several benefits. Firstly, AI has the potential to significantly speed up the drug discovery process by automating various aspects of the process. This can help to reduce the cost of drug development and improve the efficacy and safety of new drugs. AI can also help to identify new potential drug targets and optimize lead compounds, which can help to reduce the number of compounds that need to be tested in the laboratory.

However, there are also several challenges associated with using AI in drug discovery. Firstly, AI algorithms rely heavily on the data they are trained on. If the data is biased or incomplete, this can affect the accuracy of the results. Secondly, the use of AI in drug discovery raises ethical and regulatory concerns. For example, who will be responsible for the decisions made by the AI algorithms? How can the safety and efficacy of new drugs developed using AI be ensured?

The potential benefits of using AI in drug discovery and development are immense, but the risks and challenges associated with it cannot be ignored. The use of AI in drug discovery is still in its infancy, and there is a need for greater research, investment, and regulatory oversight to ensure that the benefits are maximized while minimizing the risks.

One of the significant advantages of using AI in drug discovery is the ability to analyze large amounts of data quickly and accurately. Machine learning algorithms can analyze large amounts of data, including genomic data, molecular structures, and disease characteristics, to identify potential drug targets and therapies. This process is much faster and more efficient than traditional drug discovery methods, which can take years to develop a new drug.

Another advantage of using AI is the ability to design drugs with specific properties, such as high selectivity and potency. AI algorithms can optimize the structure of a drug molecule to ensure that it binds specifically to a target protein, minimizing the risk of side effects.

The use of AI in drug discovery also has the potential to reduce costs and increase the success rate of drug development. According to a study by the consulting firm McKinsey & Company, the use of AI in drug discovery could reduce the time and cost of developing a new drug by up to 50%.

However, the use of AI in drug discovery also poses significant challenges and risks. One of the major challenges is the lack of transparency and interpretability of AI algorithms. Machine learning algorithms can be very complex, and it can be challenging to understand how they arrive at their predictions. This lack of transparency can make it difficult to validate the accuracy of the predictions and can raise ethical concerns.

Another challenge is the risk of bias in the data used to train the AI algorithms. The algorithms are only as good as the data used to train them, and if the data is biased or incomplete, the predictions of the algorithm will also be biased or incomplete. This can be especially problematic in drug development, where the data used to train the algorithms may be limited, and there may be significant variation in the genetic and environmental factors that affect the development of the disease.

Finally, there are ethical concerns associated with the use of AI in drug development. The use of AI may lead to the creation of drugs that are only accessible to those who can afford them, exacerbating existing health inequalities. There is also a risk that the use of AI in drug development could lead to the loss of jobs in the pharmaceutical industry, as the process becomes more automated.

Artificial intelligence (AI) is rapidly becoming a valuable tool in the development of new drugs and therapies for a range of diseases, including cancer and Alzheimer's. One of the primary applications of AI in drug discovery is in the identification of new drug targets, which are proteins or other molecules in the body that play a key role in the disease process. By identifying new drug targets, researchers can develop drugs that can effectively modulate the activity of these targets and, in turn, treat the disease.

AI is particularly useful in this process because it can sift through vast amounts of data from many different sources and identify patterns that might not be obvious to human researchers. This data can come from a variety of sources, including genetic data, patient medical records, and scientific literature. Machine learning algorithms can analyze this data and identify relationships between different genes, proteins, and pathways, and predict which ones might be good drug targets.

Another key area where AI is proving valuable is in the design of new drug molecules. Once a drug target has been identified, researchers must design a molecule that can effectively modulate the activity of that target while minimizing side effects. This is a challenging process that traditionally requires a great deal of trial and error, but AI is helping to streamline the process.

One approach is to use deep learning algorithms to analyze large libraries of known drug molecules and identify patterns that are associated with effective drug activity. This information can be used to design new molecules that are predicted to be more effective than those that currently exist. Another approach is to use AI to simulate the interactions between drug molecules and their targets in silico, allowing researchers to more accurately predict which molecules are likely to be effective before they are tested in the lab.

AI is also being used to improve the efficiency of clinical trials, which are a critical step in the drug development process. Clinical trials are expensive and time-consuming, and often fail to produce meaningful results. By using AI to analyze patient data and identify which patients are likely to respond well to a particular treatment, researchers can design more efficient and effective clinical trials.

One of the most exciting applications of AI in drug development is the development of personalized medicine. This approach involves tailoring treatments to individual patients based on their genetic makeup and other factors. By using AI to analyze large amounts of patient data, researchers can identify which patients are likely to respond well to a particular treatment and which are not. This allows for more targeted and effective treatments, and can reduce the likelihood of side effects.

However, there are also potential risks associated with using AI in drug development. One concern is that AI algorithms may reinforce biases that are present in the data used to train them. For example, if a training dataset contains more data on a particular group of patients, such as white males, the algorithm may be more effective at predicting outcomes for that group than for others.

There is also a risk that relying too heavily on AI in drug development could reduce the role of human intuition and creativity in the process. Drug discovery is a complex process that requires a deep understanding of biology and chemistry, as well as the ability to think creatively and come up with new ideas.

Artificial intelligence (AI) has been used to develop a range of medical technologies, from digital assistants that help patients manage their conditions to robotic surgery systems that can perform complex procedures with precision. One area where AI shows particularly promising potential is in drug discovery and development.

Traditional drug discovery involves the use of chemical libraries to find molecules that could potentially interact with a biological target, followed by rigorous testing and clinical trials to determine their efficacy and safety. This process can be time-consuming and expensive, often taking up to a decade and costing billions of dollars to bring a new drug to market.

AI-based approaches can potentially accelerate this process by identifying molecules that have the greatest likelihood of being effective at a much faster pace. One example of an AI-based drug discovery platform is Atomwise, which uses machine learning algorithms to identify potential drug candidates by analyzing vast amounts of chemical and biological data. Another example is Insilico Medicine, which uses deep learning algorithms to predict the properties of novel drug compounds.

In addition to drug discovery, AI can also be used to improve the efficiency of clinical trials. One major challenge in clinical trials is identifying patients who are most likely to respond to a particular treatment, given the heterogeneity of many diseases. AI can be used to develop predictive models that can identify biomarkers or other factors that are associated with treatment response, allowing for more targeted recruitment and more efficient trials.

AI can also be used to analyze vast amounts of medical data to identify patterns and correlations that may not be immediately apparent to human analysts. For example, the deep learning algorithm developed by Google's DeepMind has been used to analyze retinal scans and identify patients at risk of developing age-related macular degeneration.

AI-based approaches also hold promise in developing personalized therapies for patients. By analyzing genomic data, AI can help identify genetic variants that are associated with certain diseases or drug responses, allowing for the development of targeted therapies that are tailored to the individual patient.

Despite the potential benefits, there are also challenges and limitations to using AI in drug discovery and development. One major challenge is the need for large amounts of high-quality data to train machine learning algorithms. This data may not always be available or may be biased, leading to inaccurate predictions or conclusions.

Another challenge is the need to ensure the safety and efficacy of AI-based drugs. Unlike traditional drug discovery methods, AI-based drug discovery is based on machine learning algorithms that may not always be transparent in their decision-making processes. This can make it difficult to understand how and why a particular drug candidate was identified, or to identify potential biases in the training data.

The development of new drugs and therapies for diseases such as cancer and Alzheimer's has been a major challenge in the field of medicine. However, the application of artificial intelligence (AI) in drug discovery and development is changing the landscape of drug research. AI is an interdisciplinary field that focuses on the development of intelligent systems that can learn from data and make predictions based on that data. In drug discovery, AI is used to analyze large datasets, identify potential drug targets, and design new drugs.

One of the main advantages of using AI in drug discovery is the ability to analyze large amounts of data in a relatively short amount of time. For example, AI can be used to analyze the genetic data of patients with a particular disease and identify specific genes or mutations that are associated with that disease. This information can then be used to design drugs that target those specific genes or mutations.

AI can also be used to predict the effectiveness and safety of new drugs before they are tested in humans. This can significantly reduce the time and cost associated with drug development. By using AI, researchers can identify potential side effects and interactions with other drugs before they become major issues. This can help to reduce the risk of adverse reactions and improve the overall safety of new drugs.

Another advantage of using AI in drug development is the ability to identify novel drug targets. In the past, drug discovery has focused on a relatively small number of targets, such as receptors or enzymes. However, AI can analyze large datasets to identify new targets that may be involved in disease processes. This can lead to the development of drugs that target multiple pathways and have a more effective and comprehensive approach to treating diseases.

AI can also be used to design drugs that are tailored to individual patients. By analyzing a patient's genetic data and medical history, AI algorithms can identify drugs that are most likely to be effective for that particular patient. This approach, known as precision medicine, can significantly improve the effectiveness of treatments and reduce the risk of adverse reactions.

Despite the potential benefits of using AI in drug discovery and development, there are also some potential risks and challenges. One major challenge is the lack of transparency in AI algorithms. In many cases, it is difficult to understand how an AI system arrived at a particular prediction or recommendation. This can make it difficult to assess the reliability and accuracy of the results.

Another challenge is the lack of diversity in the datasets used to train AI systems. Many datasets are biased and may not accurately reflect the diversity of the population. This can lead to disparities in drug development and result in drugs that are less effective for certain populations.

There is also the risk that AI algorithms may be used inappropriately or for unethical purposes. For example, there is a risk that AI could be used to develop drugs that are designed to be addictive or to manipulate the behavior of patients.

One of the biggest advantages of using AI to develop new drugs and therapies is the speed at which the process can occur. Traditional drug development can take up to a decade and can cost billions of dollars. However, with the help of AI, researchers can accelerate the drug discovery process, reducing costs and the time it takes to bring new therapies to market. AI can help researchers sift through massive amounts of data, including genetic data, clinical trial data, and scientific literature, to find promising drug candidates and predict their potential effectiveness.

In the case of cancer, researchers are using AI to develop personalized treatment plans based on the genetic makeup of individual tumors. By analyzing the genetic data of a patient's tumor, researchers can identify the genetic mutations that are driving the growth of the cancer and select drugs that are most likely to target those mutations.

This personalized approach to treatment can be more effective than traditional chemotherapy, which can have a broad range of side effects and may not be as effective in targeting specific mutations.

In addition to speeding up drug discovery and improving treatment outcomes, AI can also help researchers identify new targets for drug development. By analyzing large datasets, AI can identify new proteins, pathways, and biomarkers that may be involved in disease progression. This knowledge can be used to develop new drugs and therapies that target these specific proteins and pathways.

Despite the many benefits of using AI in drug development, there are also some potential risks and challenges. One major concern is the lack of transparency in AI algorithms. If the algorithms used to develop new drugs are proprietary and cannot be scrutinized by other researchers, it can be difficult to assess the accuracy and reliability of the results. This lack of transparency can also lead to bias in the algorithms, which could result in drugs that are less effective for certain populations or that have unexpected side effects.

Another challenge is the need for large amounts of high-quality data to train AI algorithms. In many cases, the data needed to develop AI models is limited, which can hinder the accuracy of the predictions. There is also a risk of overfitting, where the AI model is too closely tailored to the training data and is not generalizable to new data.

Lastly, there are concerns around the ethical implications of using AI to develop new drugs and therapies. For example, there is a risk of exacerbating existing health disparities if certain populations are underrepresented in the training data or if drugs are priced too high for some patients to access.

One of the main advantages of using AI in drug discovery is the ability to speed up the process. In traditional drug development, scientists use a "trial-and-error" approach, which can take years and is often expensive. With AI, scientists can predict which compounds are most likely to be effective, saving time and resources. In fact, some estimates suggest that AI can cut the drug discovery process by as much as 75%.

Another advantage of using AI is the ability to uncover new drug targets. AI can analyze large datasets, such as genomic data and patient records, to identify patterns and correlations that would be impossible for humans to detect. By identifying new drug targets, AI could help researchers develop drugs that target specific biological pathways, making them more effective and with fewer side effects.

AI can also be used to optimize existing drugs, making them more effective and reducing the risk of side effects. By analyzing molecular structures and their interactions with the body, AI algorithms can identify potential modifications to existing drugs that could enhance their effectiveness or reduce side effects.

In addition to drug discovery, AI can also play a role in personalized medicine. By analyzing patient data, such as genomic and clinical data, AI algorithms can identify patients who are most likely to benefit from a particular treatment, reducing the risk of adverse effects and improving patient outcomes.

Despite the many benefits of using AI in drug discovery and personalized medicine, there are also potential risks and limitations to consider. One concern is the reliability of the data used to train AI algorithms. If the data is biased or incomplete, the algorithms may not be accurate or could even lead to harmful outcomes. Additionally, there is a risk of overreliance on AI, which could lead to a decrease in human intuition and creativity in the drug development process.

Another limitation is the cost of developing and implementing AI technologies. While the cost of AI technologies is decreasing, it can still be a significant investment for pharmaceutical companies and research institutions.

Finally, there is also the question of ethical and regulatory issues surrounding the use of AI in drug discovery. There is a need for clear guidelines and regulations to ensure the ethical use of AI in drug development, as well as transparency in the decision-making process.

One of the main advantages of using AI in drug discovery is the ability to analyze large amounts of data in a short amount of time. AI algorithms can process and analyze huge amounts of genomic, proteomic, and other data types that would take years for humans to complete. This has led to the development of machine learning models that can predict the efficacy of drugs, identify new targets, and create new molecules with specific properties that can be used to develop new drugs.

AI has also been used to create digital simulations of biological systems, which can be used to model drug interactions and predict the effects of different drugs on specific proteins or pathways. This can help researchers to better understand the underlying mechanisms of a disease and develop more targeted therapies.

Another benefit of using AI in drug development is the ability to reduce costs and speed up the drug discovery process. Traditional drug discovery can take years and cost billions of dollars, but by using AI to analyze data and predict drug interactions, researchers can greatly reduce the time and costs associated with drug development.

However, there are also potential risks and challenges associated with using AI in drug development. One major concern is the lack of transparency and interpretability of AI algorithms. While machine learning models can predict drug efficacy with high accuracy, it can be difficult to understand how the model arrived at its predictions. This lack of transparency can make it difficult for regulators to assess the safety and efficacy of drugs developed using AI.

Another challenge is the need for large amounts of high-quality data to train AI models. This data must be carefully curated and validated to ensure that the models are accurate and reliable. Additionally, there is the risk of bias in the data, which can lead to the development of drugs that are only effective for certain populations and not others.

There are also ethical concerns associated with using AI in drug development, particularly in the area of personalized medicine. The use of AI to develop personalized treatments based on an individual's genomic data raises questions about privacy, data ownership, and the potential for discrimination based on genetic information.

Despite these challenges, there is no doubt that AI has the potential to revolutionize the drug discovery process and lead to the development of more effective treatments for diseases such as cancer and Alzheimer's. As the technology continues to evolve and improve, researchers will be able to more effectively harness the power of AI to develop new drugs and therapies that can improve the lives of millions of people around the world.

One promising area where AI is being used to develop new drugs is in the field of drug repurposing. Drug repurposing is the process of identifying new uses for existing drugs that have already been approved by regulatory agencies. By leveraging AI algorithms and machine learning, researchers are able to analyze large amounts of data from clinical trials, electronic health records, and scientific literature to identify potential new uses for existing drugs.

AI can also help with the identification of new drug targets and the optimization of drug candidates. Traditionally, drug discovery has been a slow and expensive process that involves identifying potential drug targets, synthesizing large libraries of compounds, and testing these compounds in vitro and in vivo. AI can accelerate this process by predicting the likelihood of a given compound to be effective against a particular target, thereby narrowing down the number of compounds that need to be tested.

Moreover, AI can assist in predicting the toxicity and potential side effects of a drug candidate. By training algorithms on large datasets of adverse event reports, researchers can identify patterns that suggest potential safety concerns for new drug candidates. This can help to prevent costly and dangerous failures during clinical trials.

Additionally, AI can help to streamline clinical trial design and execution. By analyzing patient data and predicting which patients are most likely to respond to a particular drug, researchers can design more efficient and effective clinical trials. This can save time and resources, and ultimately help to get new drugs to market faster.

Despite these promising applications, there are also significant challenges to using AI for drug discovery and development. One major challenge is the availability and quality of data. While there is an abundance of data available, it is often fragmented and poorly standardized. This can make it difficult to train algorithms and make accurate predictions.

Another challenge is the lack of transparency and interpretability of many AI algorithms. While machine learning models can make accurate predictions, it is often difficult to understand why they make these predictions. This can be a major hurdle for regulatory agencies, which require a clear understanding of how drugs are developed and tested.

Furthermore, there are ethical and legal implications to consider when using AI in drug discovery and development. For example, there are concerns around the ownership and protection of data, and the potential for AI to perpetuate biases and inequalities in healthcare.

Artificial intelligence (AI) has been utilized in various industries and has had an immense impact on how people live their lives. In the field of medicine, AI has shown tremendous promise, especially in the development of new drugs and therapies for various diseases, including cancer and Alzheimer's. The increasing availability of large data sets, including genomics, proteomics, and metabolomics data, has made it possible to integrate machine learning and AI into drug discovery processes.

One of the challenges in drug discovery is the identification of new drug targets, and AI can assist in identifying these targets. AI algorithms can analyze massive amounts of data, including genomic, transcriptomic, and proteomic data, to identify targets for therapeutic intervention. The development of drugs and therapies for cancer and Alzheimer's disease requires the identification of specific targets that can be modified by drugs. The ability of AI algorithms to identify such targets has made it a powerful tool in drug discovery.

AI can also help in identifying compounds with specific biological activities that can be used in drug development. AI algorithms can identify chemical structures with specific activities, which can then be used as leads for the development of new drugs. In addition, AI can optimize these leads by modifying their chemical structures to enhance their activities and reduce their toxicity.

Furthermore, AI algorithms can be utilized in the prediction of drug toxicity. The development of new drugs is an expensive and time-consuming process, and drug failures are a significant contributor to these costs. The ability of AI algorithms to predict drug toxicity can help in reducing drug failures by identifying potential toxicity issues early in the drug development process. By predicting toxicity, drug developers can modify the chemical structure of potential drugs to reduce toxicity.

AI can also help in the repurposing of existing drugs for new indications. The ability of AI algorithms to analyze large amounts of data, including genomic, transcriptomic, and proteomic data, can help in identifying new indications for existing drugs. This approach can significantly reduce the time and cost associated with drug development, as the safety and efficacy of these drugs have already been established.

The application of AI in drug discovery is not without challenges. One of the challenges is the quality and quantity of data. AI algorithms require large amounts of high-quality data to make accurate predictions. However, the data generated in the field of drug discovery is often incomplete and noisy, which can affect the accuracy of AI predictions.

Additionally, there are ethical concerns surrounding the use of AI in drug discovery, including issues related to data privacy and informed consent.

Challenges and Limitations of AI in Drug Discovery

Despite its potential, AI-assisted drug discovery has its own set of challenges and limitations. One of the main challenges is the need for vast amounts of high-quality data, as well as the ability to process and analyze it. Another challenge is the difficulty of incorporating domain-specific knowledge, such as biological and chemical understanding, into AI models.

Furthermore, some critics have argued that AI may be better suited for optimizing existing drug candidates rather than discovering entirely new ones. This is because AI models are often based on known data and patterns, which may limit their ability to discover truly novel drug candidates that deviate significantly from existing ones.

Another limitation of AI in drug discovery is that it cannot completely replace human expertise, as it requires a combination of human and machine intelligence to fully realize its potential. In particular, experts in drug discovery are needed to help guide and interpret the AI models and to make decisions based on the results they produce.

Ethical Considerations

The use of AI in drug discovery also raises a number of ethical considerations, particularly regarding the potential for bias and discrimination. This is because the quality and quantity of the data used to train AI models can influence the results they produce, and if the data is biased or incomplete, the resulting models may also be biased or incomplete.

Additionally, the use of AI in drug discovery raises concerns about transparency and accountability, as well as the need to ensure that any resulting drugs are safe and effective for all patients. The potential for AI models to be used to target specific populations, such as those with certain genetic profiles, also raises concerns about privacy and discrimination.

As AI continues to evolve, so do the possibilities for drug discovery and development. One of the most significant benefits of AI for drug discovery is the ability to analyze vast amounts of data, including genomic and proteomic data. By analyzing large datasets, AI algorithms can identify new drug targets and potential drug candidates, helping to streamline the drug development process.

One example of how AI is being used to develop new drugs is the partnership between the British pharmaceutical company GlaxoSmithKline (GSK) and the AI startup, Exscientia. The two companies are working together to use AI to design and discover new drugs for a range of diseases. In 2017, the partnership announced that it had discovered a promising new drug candidate for the treatment of obsessive-compulsive disorder (OCD). The drug is currently undergoing preclinical development.

Another way AI is being used for drug discovery is through the creation of virtual drug screens. These screens use AI algorithms to predict the efficacy of different drug candidates. This approach can help to narrow down the field of potential drug candidates and reduce the number of expensive and time-consuming experiments required to test them.

AI is also being used to develop personalized medicine, which aims to tailor treatments to an individual's unique genetic makeup. With the help of AI, researchers can analyze genomic and proteomic data to identify the specific genetic mutations that are driving a particular disease. By understanding the underlying genetic factors that contribute to a disease, researchers can design more effective, personalized treatments that target the specific mutations responsible.

One example of this is cancer treatment. Researchers are using AI to analyze large datasets of genomic and proteomic data to identify the genetic mutations that drive different types of cancer. By understanding the specific genetic mutations that are responsible for a particular cancer, researchers can design personalized treatments that target those mutations.

AI is also being used to analyze medical images, such as MRI and CT scans, to help identify and diagnose diseases. By analyzing medical images, AI algorithms can detect subtle changes in tissue and help identify early signs of disease. This can help to facilitate earlier diagnosis and more effective treatments.

Despite the many potential benefits of using AI for drug discovery and development, there are also several risks and challenges to consider. One concern is the potential for bias in the data used to train AI algorithms. If the data used to train the algorithms is biased, this could result in inaccurate predictions and flawed drug candidates. It is important for researchers to carefully consider the quality and diversity of the data used to train AI algorithms to ensure that the algorithms are robust and unbiased.

Another risk is the potential for AI to be used to automate unethical or illegal practices, such as the creation of designer drugs or the manipulation of clinical trial data. It is important for researchers to establish ethical guidelines and regulations to ensure that AI is used for the benefit of patients and society as a whole.

There are concerns about the potential impact of AI on employment in the pharmaceutical industry. As AI is increasingly used to automate drug discovery and development, it is possible that many traditional roles in the pharmaceutical industry will become obsolete. It is important for the industry to anticipate these changes and develop strategies to retrain and redeploy workers in other areas.

In recent years, there has been a rapid increase in the use of artificial intelligence (AI) to develop new drugs and therapies for a range of diseases, including cancer and Alzheimer's. One key benefit of using AI in drug discovery is its ability to accelerate the drug development process, which traditionally can take many years and cost billions of dollars.

AI systems can analyze vast amounts of data to identify new drug targets, predict drug efficacy and toxicity, and optimize drug design. For example, machine learning algorithms can be trained to analyze large databases of genomic and proteomic data to identify new drug targets that are specific to a particular disease. These AI systems can also simulate the molecular interactions between drugs and their targets, which can help researchers optimize drug design and predict drug efficacy and toxicity.

One promising application of AI in drug discovery is the development of personalized medicine. With the help of AI systems, it is possible to analyze an individual's genetic information to identify specific mutations that are driving their disease. This information can then be used to develop personalized drug therapies that are tailored to the individual's specific genetic profile.

In addition to accelerating the drug development process and enabling the development of personalized medicine, AI also has the potential to significantly reduce the cost of drug development. By optimizing drug design and predicting drug efficacy and toxicity, AI can help pharmaceutical companies reduce the number of failed drug trials and increase the success rate of new drug development.

Despite these potential benefits, there are also some significant challenges and risks associated with using AI in drug discovery. One major challenge is the lack of transparency and interpretability of AI systems. In many cases, it is not clear how these systems arrive at their conclusions or what factors they are taking into account when making predictions. This lack of transparency can make it difficult to validate the results of AI systems and ensure that they are producing accurate and reliable predictions.

Another significant risk associated with using AI in drug discovery is the potential for unintended consequences. For example, AI systems may identify drug targets that are highly effective at treating a particular disease but also have off-target effects that cause unintended harm to the patient. In addition, AI systems may be biased towards certain types of drugs or certain disease targets, which could lead to the development of drugs that are less effective or less safe than they appear.

Despite these challenges and risks, the use of AI in drug discovery is likely to become increasingly common in the coming years. As AI systems continue to improve and become more reliable and transparent, they have the potential to revolutionize the drug development process and enable the development of highly effective and personalized drug therapies for a range of diseases. However, it will be important to carefully evaluate the risks and benefits of using AI in drug discovery and to develop robust systems for validating and testing the predictions of these systems.

Artificial intelligence (AI) has revolutionized the way we approach scientific research, and it is now playing a major role in drug discovery and development. By utilizing machine learning algorithms and advanced data analytics, researchers can quickly analyze large datasets and identify patterns that could lead to the development of new drugs and therapies. In the case of cancer, AI has the potential to identify new targets and biomarkers for precision medicine and personalized therapies. Similarly, in the case of Alzheimer's, AI can help researchers identify potential drug candidates that could target specific pathways in the brain that are responsible for the development of the disease.

One of the biggest challenges in drug development is identifying the right targets and biomarkers to focus on. With the help of AI, researchers can now analyze large datasets that contain information on the molecular mechanisms of diseases and identify potential targets and biomarkers that were previously unknown. This has led to the development of new drugs and therapies that target specific pathways and molecules that are involved in the development of diseases such as cancer and Alzheimer's.

AI has also enabled the development of more efficient drug discovery and development processes. For example, AI algorithms can be used to predict the toxicity of new drug candidates and reduce the number of potential drug candidates that need to be tested in clinical trials. This can save time and money, and speed up the process of drug discovery and development.

Another major advantage of using AI in drug development is the ability to personalize treatments for patients. By analyzing a patient's genetic makeup and other relevant data, AI algorithms can identify potential drug candidates that are most likely to be effective for that particular patient. This can lead to more effective treatments and better outcomes for patients.

Despite these potential benefits, there are also some risks associated with using AI in drug development. One of the biggest concerns is the potential for bias in the algorithms used to analyze the data. If the algorithms are not properly designed, they could lead to inaccurate predictions and recommendations. Additionally, there is a risk of overreliance on AI and a reduction in the role of human experts in the drug development process. This could lead to a lack of transparency and accountability, as well as a potential loss of valuable insights and expertise.

As artificial intelligence continues to improve, it is becoming more and more possible to use it to develop new drugs and therapies for diseases like cancer and Alzheimer's. AI can be used to sift through vast amounts of data, identifying patterns and correlations that may not be apparent to human researchers. This can lead to the discovery of new drug targets, as well as the development of more personalized treatment plans.

One example of how AI is being used in drug development is through the use of generative models. These models use machine learning algorithms to generate new drug candidates that are structurally similar to existing drugs. Researchers can then test these candidates in the lab to see if they have potential therapeutic effects. By using AI to generate these candidates, researchers can potentially speed up the drug development process and identify new treatments that may not have been discovered otherwise.

Another way that AI is being used in drug development is through the use of predictive analytics. Researchers can use machine learning algorithms to analyze large datasets of patient information and identify patterns that may be indicative of disease. By identifying these patterns, researchers can better understand the underlying mechanisms of disease and develop targeted therapies to address them. This approach is particularly promising for diseases like cancer, where a personalized treatment approach is often necessary to achieve optimal outcomes.

AI can also be used to improve clinical trials, which are a critical part of the drug development process. By using predictive analytics, researchers can better identify which patients are most likely to respond to a particular treatment, reducing the time and resources needed to conduct clinical trials. Additionally, AI can help researchers better identify potential side effects of drugs, which can help ensure patient safety.

Despite the potential benefits of using AI in drug development, there are also significant challenges to overcome. One of the biggest challenges is data quality. In order for machine learning algorithms to be effective, they need access to large amounts of high-quality data. However, much of the data that is currently available is incomplete, inaccurate, or biased, which can limit the effectiveness of AI algorithms.

Another challenge is the need for collaboration between different stakeholders in the drug development process. AI is most effective when it can be applied across multiple stages of the drug development process, from target identification to clinical trials. This requires collaboration between researchers, clinicians, and drug companies, as well as the development of open data standards that can be used across different organizations.

Finally, there are also ethical considerations to take into account when using AI in drug development. For example, there is a risk that AI algorithms could reinforce existing biases or lead to over-reliance on automated decision-making, which could have negative consequences for patient care. It is therefore important for researchers to carefully consider the potential ethical implications of their work and take steps to mitigate any potential risks.

In conclusion, the use of artificial intelligence in drug discovery and development has the potential to revolutionize the healthcare industry. AI algorithms can help identify potential drug targets, design new molecules, and optimize drug properties. The ability of AI to analyze large amounts of data and identify complex patterns can also aid in the discovery of new therapeutic uses for existing drugs.

In the case of diseases like cancer and Alzheimer's, AI can help accelerate the development of new therapies by identifying potential targets and drug candidates, predicting clinical outcomes, and optimizing treatment regimens. The use of AI in these areas has already yielded promising results, with several AI-designed drugs and therapies already in clinical trials.

However, there are also potential risks and challenges associated with the use of AI in drug development. AI algorithms may be biased by the data used to train them, and there is a risk that the algorithms may overlook important biological or clinical factors. Additionally, the development and regulation of AI-designed drugs and therapies will need to be carefully monitored to ensure that they are safe and effective for patients.

Overall, the use of AI in drug development is an exciting area of research that has the potential to greatly improve patient outcomes for a wide range of diseases. However, it will be important to balance the potential benefits with the potential risks and challenges, and to continue to develop and refine AI algorithms and techniques to ensure that they are robust, accurate, and effective.

CHAPTER V

How can we use robotics to explore and colonize other planets in our solar system?"

Introduction:

Robotic exploration of space is an essential aspect of the search for new worlds and habitats for human beings. While human space travel has played a vital role in space exploration, robots offer several advantages over humans, including their resilience to the harsh environments of space and their ability to carry out repetitive and dangerous tasks with high precision. Robotics has contributed significantly to space exploration, from the first unmanned mission to the moon to the ongoing exploration of Mars. This paper explores how robotics can be used to explore and colonize other planets in our solar system.

Robotic Missions to Other Planets:

Robotic missions have been essential in studying other planets in our solar system. These missions involve sending remotely operated robots to other planets to collect data and take images. The first successful robotic mission to another planet was the Mariner 2 mission in 1962, which sent a spacecraft to Venus to study its atmosphere and magnetic field. Since then, several missions have been carried out, including the ongoing Mars exploration missions by NASA and other space agencies.

The Mars Exploration Program:

NASA's Mars Exploration Program is one of the most ambitious robotic exploration programs in history. The program aims to explore Mars in detail to determine its habitability and to search for evidence of past or present life. The program has used several robotic spacecraft, including the Curiosity rover, which landed on Mars in 2012 and has been exploring the planet ever since. The Perseverance rover, launched in 2020, is the latest addition to the program and aims to collect and analyze rock samples that could provide valuable insights into the planet's geological history and potential habitability.

The Use of Robotics in Colonizing Other Planets:

The colonization of other planets is a critical goal for space exploration, and robotics can play a crucial role in this endeavor. Robots can carry out tasks that are too dangerous or impractical for humans, such as mining and construction. The use of robots in colonizing other planets would also help reduce costs since robots do not require life support systems, food, and water, as human missions do.

One of the key challenges in colonizing other planets is the need to build habitats that can sustain human life. Robotic technologies, such as 3D printing, could be used to construct habitats on other planets. NASA is currently exploring the use of a 3D-printed habitat on Mars, which could be built using locally available materials. Robots could also be used to mine resources on other planets, which could be used for construction and other purposes.

The Importance of Autonomous Robotics in Space Exploration:

Autonomous robotics plays a crucial role in space exploration since it enables robots to operate independently in challenging environments. Autonomous robots can use sensors and artificial intelligence to make decisions and carry out tasks without human intervention. This technology is particularly important in situations where communication delays between Earth and the robots are significant.

The use of autonomous robots in space exploration has been demonstrated in several missions, including the Mars Exploration Program. For example, the Curiosity rover can perform several tasks autonomously, including driving, collecting and analyzing samples, and operating its robotic arm.

Challenges and Limitations:

The use of robotics in space exploration is not without its challenges and limitations. One of the main challenges is the harsh environment of space, which can cause damage to robots and their electronic components. Radiation exposure is another significant challenge since it can damage electronic components and affect the performance of robots.

The limited energy supply is another constraint that limits the capabilities of robotic systems. The use of solar panels to power robotic systems can be limited by the amount of sunlight available. Another significant limitation is the high cost of developing and launching robotic systems, which can limit the number of missions that can be carried out

Robotic exploration of other planets has been a topic of interest for several decades. As our technology advances, our ability to explore and ultimately colonize other planets has increased. The use of robotics in space exploration has been instrumental in paving the way for humans to eventually travel to other planets.

One of the most significant challenges in space exploration is the distance between Earth and other planets. For example, Mars, which is considered the most hospitable planet for humans after Earth, is about 140 million miles away from Earth. This distance poses numerous challenges in terms of communication, energy, and resources.

To overcome these challenges, robotics has been used to develop unmanned spacecraft that can be sent to explore and colonize other planets. These spacecraft are equipped with sensors, cameras, and other instruments that enable them to collect data and information about the planet. This information is then transmitted back to Earth, where it can be analyzed and used to plan future missions.

One example of a successful robotic mission to another planet is the Mars rover program. NASA has sent four rovers to Mars, including the Sojourner, Spirit, Opportunity, and Curiosity. These rovers have been able to collect valuable information about the Martian environment, including its geology, atmosphere, and potential for supporting life.

In addition to rovers, robotics has also been used to develop other types of spacecraft for space exploration. For example, the Mars Reconnaissance Orbiter (MRO) is an unmanned spacecraft that was sent to Mars in 2005. The MRO is equipped with cameras, spectrometers, and other instruments that enable it to study the Martian atmosphere, geology, and weather patterns. The MRO has been instrumental in identifying potential landing sites for future manned missions to Mars.

Another use of robotics in space exploration is the development of autonomous systems that can operate independently in space. For example, the Space Robotics Project is a joint project between NASA and the Japanese space agency JAXA to develop robots that can work together to perform tasks such as assembling structures in space. These robots are designed to be self-sufficient and able to operate in harsh space environments without human intervention.

One of the most exciting uses of robotics in space exploration is the development of technologies that can be used to colonize other planets. For example, robots could be used to construct habitats on other planets, which could be used to house humans as they explore and study the planet. In addition, robots could be used to mine resources on other planets, which could be used to sustain human life on the planet.

However, there are also significant challenges to using robotics to explore and colonize other planets. For example, the harsh environments on other planets can be very challenging for robotic systems. Extreme temperatures, radiation, and lack of oxygen are just a few of the challenges that robotic systems must be designed to overcome.

In addition, the cost of developing and launching robotic spacecraft can be very high. This cost is a significant barrier to expanding our exploration and colonization efforts to other planets.

Despite these challenges, the use of robotics in space exploration has the potential to revolutionize our understanding of the universe and enable humans to travel and colonize other planets. The development of new and advanced robotic systems will be essential to making this vision a reality.

Exploration of other planets in our solar system, especially Mars, has become a major focus for space agencies and private companies alike. However, sending humans to other planets is a complicated and risky endeavor. That is where robotics can play a crucial role in exploring and colonizing other planets in our solar system.

Robotics can serve as a precursor to human missions and enable us to study and learn more about the target planet, its environment, and resources.

There are a few key ways in which robotics can be used to explore and colonize other planets. First, robots can be sent ahead of human missions to prepare the site for human arrival. For example, they could set up habitats, resource extraction equipment, and communication systems. This could help to make human missions safer and more efficient.

Second, robots can be used to collect data and samples from the planet. This can be done through a variety of means, including rovers, landers, and even drones. These robots can collect soil samples, take images and measurements, and study the environment and conditions on the planet. The data collected by these robots can help scientists learn more about the planet and its potential for supporting life, and can inform future missions.

Third, robots can be used to build infrastructure on the planet. For example, they could be used to build roads, runways, and even habitats for humans. This would make it easier and more cost-effective to establish a human presence on the planet.

One of the biggest challenges in using robotics to explore and colonize other planets is the communication delay. Since the planets are so far away, there is a significant delay in the time it takes for signals to travel to and from the robots on the planet. This delay can make it difficult to operate the robots in real-time, which is necessary for many tasks. To overcome this challenge, researchers are developing new algorithms and software that enable robots to operate autonomously, with minimal human input.

Another challenge is the harsh environment on other planets, which can be challenging for robotic systems. For example, the extreme cold and radiation on Mars can damage electronics and other sensitive components. To overcome this challenge, researchers are developing new materials and designs that can withstand the harsh conditions on other planets.

Robots are not just useful in space exploration, but also in establishing and maintaining extraterrestrial settlements. As technology continues to advance, it is likely that robots will play an increasingly important role in the colonization of other planets.

One of the main advantages of using robots in space is that they can be designed to operate autonomously for extended periods of time. This means that they can be sent ahead of humans to set up infrastructure and prepare for human habitation. For example, robots could be used to build habitats, extract and purify water from ice, and mine for minerals that can be used in construction and other applications.

In addition to their ability to operate autonomously, robots can also be designed to withstand harsh conditions such as extreme temperatures, radiation, and low gravity. For example, the Mars rovers Curiosity and Perseverance are equipped with specialized wheels and suspension systems that allow them to navigate over rough terrain and climb steep slopes.

One area of robotics research that is particularly relevant to space exploration is the development of humanoid robots that can perform tasks traditionally done by humans. For example, a humanoid robot could be used to repair equipment, conduct scientific experiments, and perform maintenance on infrastructure. By using humanoid robots, we could potentially reduce the number of humans needed for a mission, thereby lowering costs and minimizing the risks associated with human spaceflight.

Another area of robotics research that is important for space exploration is the development of swarm robotics, which involves the use of large numbers of small robots working together to accomplish a task. In space, swarm robotics could be used to explore large areas of a planet's surface or to perform complex tasks that would be difficult for a single robot to complete on its own.

As we continue to explore the possibilities of using robotics to explore and colonize other planets in our solar system, there are many challenges that we must overcome. One of the primary challenges is developing robots that are capable of operating in the harsh environments of other planets. For example, the atmosphere on Mars is much thinner than that of Earth, and the planet's surface is subject to intense radiation from the sun. These conditions make it difficult for robots to operate, and we must develop new technologies to ensure that our robots are capable of functioning in these environments.

Another challenge is developing robots that are capable of performing complex tasks. To successfully colonize other planets, we need robots that can perform a wide range of tasks, from mining resources to building habitats. This requires developing robots that are capable of performing intricate movements and manipulating objects with precision. We also need robots that can operate autonomously, without human intervention, for extended periods of time. This will require advanced artificial intelligence and machine learning technologies.

In addition to developing robots that are capable of operating in harsh environments and performing complex tasks, we also need to ensure that these robots are reliable and safe. One of the risks of using robots to explore and colonize other planets is the possibility of a malfunction that could result in damage to the robot or to the environment. We need to develop robots that are equipped with redundant systems to ensure that they can continue to operate in the event of a failure. We also need to ensure that the robots are equipped with fail-safe mechanisms that will prevent them from causing harm to humans or to the environment.

Another important consideration is the ethical implications of using robots to explore and colonize other planets. As we push the boundaries of what is possible with robotics, we need to ensure that we are not causing harm to other living beings. For example, we need to consider the impact that our robots may have on any indigenous life that we may encounter on other planets. We also need to consider the potential impact of our actions on the environment of these planets.

Despite these challenges, the potential benefits of using robotics to explore and colonize other planets are vast. By using robots, we can gather valuable data about other planets that can help us better understand the formation and evolution of our solar system. We can also search for signs of life on other planets, which could provide important insights into the origins of life in the universe. And if we are successful in colonizing other planets, we can open up new opportunities for human exploration and settlement, which could lead to significant advances in science, technology, and human culture.

As humans continue to explore and study our solar system, the use of robotics has become increasingly important. Robots are able to gather data in hostile environments, such as the extreme temperatures and atmospheric conditions found on other planets, without risking human lives. Additionally, robots are able to work for long periods of time without the need for rest or food, making them ideal for long-term missions. This has led to the development of a variety of robotic systems that can be used to explore and potentially colonize other planets in our solar system.

One important aspect of robotic exploration and colonization is the ability to navigate through harsh terrain. Planets such as Mars are rocky, with uneven surfaces and deep crevices that can pose significant challenges to exploration. Robotic systems such as the Mars Rover have been designed with the ability to traverse such terrain, using specialized wheels and suspension systems to maintain balance and mobility. In addition, robots designed for exploration can be equipped with sensors and cameras that allow them to detect obstacles and hazards in their path, further increasing their ability to navigate through challenging terrain.

Another important consideration for robotic exploration and colonization is the ability to extract resources from other planets. This is particularly important for long-term missions, where resources such as water and minerals can be used to sustain human life. Robots are able to carry out a variety of tasks related to resource extraction, such as drilling for water and minerals, processing raw materials, and performing chemical analysis to determine the composition of the planet's surface. By extracting resources and processing them into usable forms, robots can help to provide a sustainable source of resources for human colonists.

In addition to their ability to navigate challenging terrain and extract resources, robots can also be designed to perform a variety of other tasks related to planetary exploration and colonization. For example, robots can be used to build structures such as habitats and launch sites, as well as to carry out maintenance and repair tasks. They can also be used to conduct scientific experiments and gather data on the planet's geology, atmosphere, and other key features.

As the use of robotics for planetary exploration and colonization continues to evolve, there are also several key challenges that must be addressed. One of the biggest challenges is the need for reliable communication systems, particularly for missions that are far from Earth. As robots become more sophisticated and autonomous, they will need to be able to communicate effectively with human controllers in order to receive instructions and transmit data. Another key challenge is the need for advanced power systems that can sustain robots for long periods of time. While current solar and battery technologies are effective for short-term missions, they may not be sufficient for long-term exploration and colonization.

As space exploration and colonization continue to be a topic of interest and research, the use of robotics in these endeavors is becoming increasingly important. With robots, we can explore areas that are too dangerous or difficult for humans to reach, gather data and samples, and build infrastructure for future missions. In the case of colonizing other planets, robots can be used to build habitats, mine resources, and perform tasks that may be too dangerous or impractical for humans to do.

One of the biggest advantages of using robots in space exploration is their ability to operate autonomously, reducing the need for constant human intervention. This is especially important in cases where there is a communication delay between Earth and the remote location, as it can take several minutes for a signal to travel to and from the robot. As a result, robots are designed to be highly autonomous and able to operate with minimal human intervention. This means they can continue to work even if there is a communication failure or other issue that prevents humans from providing real-time guidance.

Another advantage of using robots in space exploration is their ability to withstand harsh environments. Robots can be designed to operate in extreme temperatures, radiation, and other challenging conditions that would be impossible for humans to tolerate. This means they can be used to explore areas of other planets that may be too dangerous or inhospitable for human life.

In addition, robots can be used to build and maintain infrastructure for future human missions. For example, robots could be used to mine resources and build habitats, which would reduce the amount of resources that need to be transported from Earth. This could significantly reduce the cost and complexity of future missions, as it would eliminate the need for large-scale supply missions to bring materials and resources to the remote location.

Robots can also be used to perform scientific research and gather data in remote locations. For example, robots could be used to explore the deep oceans of other planets, collect samples, and conduct experiments. This data could be used to learn more about the geology, chemistry, and biology of these planets, as well as to search for signs of life.

However, there are also challenges associated with using robots in space exploration. One of the biggest challenges is the cost and complexity of designing and building robots that can operate in extreme conditions. In addition, robots must be designed to be highly reliable and durable, as they may need to operate for extended periods of time without maintenance or repair.

Another challenge is the difficulty of remotely controlling robots in real-time. As mentioned earlier, there is a significant communication delay between Earth and remote locations, which can make it difficult to provide real-time guidance to the robot. As a result, robots must be designed to operate autonomously and make decisions on their own, which can be difficult to achieve in complex or unpredictable environments.

Finally, there is also the risk of contamination when using robots to explore other planets. It is important to ensure that the robot does not carry any microorganisms from Earth that could potentially contaminate the remote location and interfere with scientific research.

Despite these challenges, the use of robots in space exploration and colonization is an important area of research and development. With continued advancements in robotics technology, we can expect to see more sophisticated and capable robots being used in future space missions, which will enable us to explore and colonize other planets in our solar system and beyond.

As the use of robots in space exploration becomes more prevalent, researchers are continuously developing new technologies to make robotic missions more efficient and productive. One area of research is in the development of autonomous robots that can operate on planets without direct human control. These robots will be able to carry out tasks on their own, without constant communication with Earth, allowing for longer missions and more scientific discoveries.

One example of autonomous robots in development is the Mars Science Laboratory (MSL) rover, Curiosity. Curiosity is the largest rover ever sent to another planet and is equipped with numerous scientific instruments, including a drill for sampling rocks and a laser for analyzing their composition. Curiosity is also able to navigate autonomously over the Martian terrain, using onboard cameras and software to make decisions about where to go and how to get there.

Another area of research is in the development of swarms of robots that can work together to complete tasks. These robots would be smaller and less complex than larger, autonomous rovers, but would work in large numbers to explore and map areas of interest. The European Space Agency (ESA) has developed a prototype swarm of robots, known as the Droplets, which can move across a surface and interact with one another to complete tasks such as pushing objects or forming patterns.

In addition to their use in exploration, robots may also play a role in the eventual colonization of other planets. One area of research is in the development of robots that can construct and maintain habitats on other planets. NASA's In Situ Fabricator (ISF) is a robot designed to build structures using in situ resources, such as the Martian regolith. By mining the regolith for materials and using additive manufacturing techniques, the ISF could potentially build structures that would serve as habitats for human colonists.

Robots may also play a critical role in the eventual mining of resources on other planets. Asteroids in particular are rich in metals such as platinum, gold, and silver, and robots could be used to extract these resources. The Japan Aerospace Exploration Agency (JAXA) has sent the Hayabusa2 mission to asteroid Ryugu, which will use robots to gather samples and return them to Earth.

However, the use of robots in space exploration and colonization also poses numerous challenges. One of the major challenges is the development of robots that can operate in extreme environments, such as the high radiation and temperature fluctuations on the surface of Mars. Another challenge is the development of reliable and efficient communication systems, as communication delays between Earth and other planets can be significant.

In addition, there are ethical considerations that must be taken into account when using robots for space exploration and colonization. One concern is the impact of robotic missions on the environment of other planets. The contamination of other planets with Earth microbes could potentially harm any native life that may exist. Another concern is the potential replacement of human exploration with robotic exploration, which could limit opportunities for human exploration and scientific discovery.

Exploring and colonizing other planets in the solar system is an exciting prospect, but it comes with significant challenges. One of the most significant challenges is developing robotics that can function autonomously in harsh and unpredictable environments. This includes developing robots that can adapt to a variety of terrains, withstand extreme temperatures, and function in the absence of an atmosphere.

One potential solution is to design robots that are modular and adaptable. Modular robots can be reconfigured into different shapes and sizes, allowing them to navigate different terrains and perform a variety of tasks. This could be especially useful on a planet like Mars, where the terrain is highly variable and unpredictable. Adaptable robots, meanwhile, can adjust their behavior and decision-making algorithms based on changing conditions, making them better equipped to deal with unexpected events.

Another challenge is developing robots that can operate for extended periods without human intervention. This requires developing robots that can operate autonomously, with the ability to recharge or repair themselves as needed. In addition, robots will need to be able to carry out complex tasks without human intervention, such as drilling for water, collecting samples, and building infrastructure.

One approach to achieving this is to develop robots that can make use of local resources. For example, robots could be designed to extract water from ice deposits or process minerals to generate oxygen for fuel. This would allow robots to operate for extended periods without requiring regular resupply missions.

Another approach is to develop robots that can work in teams. By working together, robots can share resources and knowledge, allowing them to accomplish more complex tasks than they could individually. This could be especially useful in situations where time is of the essence, such as during emergency repairs or scientific experiments.

In addition to developing robots, there are a number of other technological challenges that must be overcome to enable the exploration and colonization of other planets. One of the most significant is the development of sustainable and reliable energy sources. Solar power is one option, but this is limited by the length of daylight on some planets. Nuclear power could be a viable alternative, but it presents significant safety concerns.

Another challenge is developing the infrastructure necessary to support human habitation. This includes designing habitats that can withstand harsh environments and provide a comfortable living space for astronauts. It also involves developing systems for food production, waste management, and water recycling.

There are a number of ethical and legal considerations that must be taken into account when exploring and colonizing other planets. For example, there are questions around the ownership of resources and the potential impact of colonization on indigenous life. These issues must be carefully considered and addressed to ensure that exploration and colonization are carried out in a responsible and sustainable manner.

Furthermore, the use of robots in space exploration offers numerous advantages over human-led missions. For one, robots are not limited by the same constraints that humans are. For instance, they do not need to breathe air or consume food and water, making them more adaptable to the harsh conditions in space. Additionally, robots can work around the clock without getting tired, whereas humans need rest and sleep, limiting the amount of work that can be done in a given day.

Robots are also able to take risks and survive in conditions that would be impossible for humans. For example, they can withstand high levels of radiation, extreme temperatures, and harsh environments that humans cannot survive in without proper protection. Furthermore, robots can be programmed to carry out tasks that are too dangerous for humans, such as inspecting the surface of a planet that may be home to toxic chemicals or other hazards.

As technology continues to advance, the use of robots in space exploration is becoming more prevalent. In recent years, there have been a number of successful robotic missions to Mars, including the Mars Exploration Rovers and the Mars Science Laboratory. These robots have allowed scientists to explore the surface of the planet in unprecedented detail, providing valuable information about its geology, climate, and potential for supporting life.

Looking ahead, there are numerous challenges that need to be addressed if we are to continue using robots to explore and colonize other planets in our solar system. One of the biggest challenges is developing robots that are able to operate autonomously for long periods of time without human intervention. Additionally, robots will need to be able to navigate difficult terrain and handle a range of tasks, from drilling into the surface of a planet to constructing habitats for humans.

Robotic missions have played a critical role in our exploration of other planets in our solar system. In the past few decades, rovers like Spirit, Opportunity, and Curiosity have made tremendous contributions to our understanding of Mars. These robots have conducted geological surveys, analyzed soil samples, and sent back detailed images of the planet's surface. The success of these missions has sparked interest in using robotics to explore and eventually colonize other planets.

One of the key challenges of exploring other planets is the harsh environment. Planetary surfaces can be incredibly rugged and inhospitable to life as we know it. Extreme temperatures, high radiation levels, and a lack of breathable air make it impossible for humans to explore these environments without protection. Robotics provides a way to explore these environments without putting humans in harm's way.

In order to explore and colonize other planets, robots need to be able to navigate and interact with the environment. This requires advanced sensors, navigation systems, and actuators that can manipulate the environment. The development of these systems is a major area of research in robotics. There are many challenges associated with designing robots that can operate in harsh environments. For example, robots need to be able to move over rough terrain, navigate steep slopes, and avoid obstacles. They also need to be able to operate in low light conditions, and deal with temperature extremes.

One promising approach to addressing these challenges is the development of biomimetic robots. Biomimetic robots are inspired by nature and designed to mimic the behavior of living organisms. These robots are often designed to operate in extreme environments, and they use a range of sensors and actuators that are modeled on biological systems. For example, researchers have developed robots that can move like snakes, or climb like geckos. These robots are well-suited to exploring planetary surfaces, and they could be used to collect samples and conduct detailed surveys of other planets.

Another approach to exploring other planets is the use of autonomous robots. Autonomous robots are able to make decisions and carry out tasks without human intervention. This makes them well-suited to operating in remote and hostile environments. Autonomous robots have already been used to explore other planets. For example, the Mars rovers have been programmed to carry out a range of tasks, from collecting soil samples to drilling into rocks. These robots are capable of making decisions based on their environment, and they can carry out complex tasks without human input.

The use of robots for space exploration has already proven to be highly successful. However, there are still many challenges that need to be addressed. One of the biggest challenges is the communication delay between Earth and other planets. This delay can make it difficult to operate robots in real-time, and it can limit the complexity of tasks that can be carried out remotely. Another challenge is the need for more advanced sensors and instruments that can provide more detailed information about the environment.

The use of robotics in space exploration has greatly expanded the reach of human exploration beyond the boundaries of Earth. With advancements in technology, we have seen the development of more sophisticated robots and autonomous systems that can operate with minimal human intervention. Robots are a valuable asset in space exploration, allowing us to perform tasks that would be difficult or impossible for humans to do.

One significant area where robotics has been applied is in the exploration of other planets in our solar system. Robotic missions have provided valuable insights into the geology, atmosphere, and conditions on other planets. For instance, the Mars Exploration Rovers, Spirit and Opportunity, launched in 2003, were some of the most successful robotic missions to Mars. They were designed to last for three months but continued to send data back to Earth for years, providing valuable information about the Martian environment. Similarly, the Curiosity rover, launched in 2011, continues to operate on Mars, providing scientists with new data and discoveries.

The use of robotics has also expanded our understanding of other celestial bodies in our solar system. For example, in 2014, the European Space Agency's Rosetta spacecraft successfully landed a robotic probe, Philae, on the surface of a comet. This was the first time a spacecraft had landed on a comet, providing valuable information about the composition and structure of comets.

Another area where robotics can be applied is in the colonization of other planets. Currently, human exploration of other planets is limited by the high cost, technological limitations, and long travel times. However, with the use of robotics, we can remotely explore and establish bases on other planets, paving the way for future human settlement.

For example, NASA's Mars 2020 mission aims to land a rover on Mars to search for signs of past microbial life, collect rock samples, and conduct experiments to prepare for human exploration. The Mars Sample Return mission, expected to launch in the late 2020s, will collect rock and soil samples from Mars and return them to Earth, allowing scientists to study them in detail.

Robotics is also being used in the development of sustainable living on other planets. One example is the BioRock project, which explores the use of genetically modified cyanobacteria to create a sustainable ecosystem on Mars. The project involves using robotics to simulate and test the growth of these bacteria in simulated Martian environments.

The main advantage of using robots for space exploration is their ability to operate in extreme environments without risking human life. Robots can survive harsh conditions such as extreme temperatures, radiation, and pressure that would be fatal to humans. Therefore, they can be used to explore and gather information about planets and moons that humans cannot reach.

One example of a robotic mission that has been successful in exploring a planet is the Mars Rover mission. The mission was launched by NASA in 1996, and it sent two rovers, Spirit and Opportunity, to explore the surface of Mars. The rovers were equipped with various instruments such as cameras, spectrometers, and rock abrasion tools to examine the geology and atmosphere of the planet. The mission provided valuable information about the planet's past and potential for life, and it demonstrated the effectiveness of using robotics for space exploration.

Another advantage of using robots for space exploration is their versatility. Robots can be designed to perform a wide range of tasks such as drilling, sampling, analyzing, and building structures. This makes them ideal for carrying out various activities required for establishing a human presence on other planets, such as mining resources, constructing habitats, and producing oxygen.

Robotic exploration is also cost-effective compared to manned missions. The cost of sending a robot to a planet is much lower than sending humans, as robots require less life support equipment and are not subject to the same safety concerns as humans. Additionally, robots can operate for extended periods without maintenance, which reduces the need for frequent resupply missions.

As technology continues to advance, robots will become more capable of carrying out complex tasks and operating autonomously. Autonomous robots will be able to make decisions based on their environment, which will enable them to explore more efficiently and effectively.

In conclusion, robotics offers a tremendous opportunity to explore and colonize other planets in our solar system. Advancements in robotics technology have already provided scientists with powerful tools to gather data and conduct experiments on Mars, and these technologies will only continue to improve in the coming years. By utilizing robots that are able to operate in extreme environments and adapt to different challenges, we can learn more about our solar system and explore new possibilities for human colonization.

However, there are still many challenges that must be addressed before human colonization of other planets becomes a reality. The development of more sophisticated and capable robots, along with the continued refinement of communication and propulsion technologies, will be necessary to make interplanetary travel and settlement possible. Additionally, ethical considerations surrounding the potential impact of colonization on extraterrestrial environments must also be addressed.

Despite these challenges, the potential benefits of space exploration and colonization are significant, both in terms of scientific discovery and human progress. Through continued investment in robotics technology and space exploration, we may one day unlock new frontiers in the search for knowledge and human expansion.

CHAPTER VI

How can we overcome the technological and logistical challenges of sending humans to Mars and beyond?

Introduction:

Space exploration has come a long way since the first human landed on the moon. In recent years, the focus has shifted towards more ambitious goals, such as sending humans to Mars and beyond. This research paper will explore the current state of space travel and the challenges that need to be overcome to achieve this goal.

Current State of Space Travel:

The current state of space travel is centered around the International Space Station (ISS), a collaboration between five space agencies - NASA, Roscosmos, JAXA, ESA, and CSA. The ISS has been continuously inhabited by humans since November 2000, and serves as a platform for conducting scientific experiments, testing technologies, and preparing for future missions. In addition, several private companies, such as SpaceX and Blue Origin, have developed reusable rockets and spacecraft, which have significantly reduced the cost of launching payloads into space.

Challenges of Sending Humans to Mars and Beyond:

Sending humans to Mars and beyond presents significant technological and logistical challenges. One of the primary challenges is developing a spacecraft that can transport humans safely over such long distances. The journey to Mars can take anywhere from 150 to 300 days, depending on the alignment of the planets, and the spacecraft must be equipped to provide life support systems, protection from radiation, and a means for recycling waste.

Another significant challenge is landing on the surface of Mars. The Martian atmosphere is much thinner than Earth's, which makes it difficult to slow down the spacecraft during the descent. In addition, the terrain on Mars is much rougher than the Moon's, which means that the landing system must be able to handle the rocky terrain and dust storms that can occur.

Finally, sustaining human life on Mars presents its own set of challenges. The Martian environment is hostile to life, with temperatures ranging from -195°C to 20°C, a lack of oxygen, and high levels of radiation. Any human settlement on Mars would need to be completely self-sufficient, with its own food and water sources, as well as energy generation and waste management systems.

Future of Space Travel:

Despite these challenges, there is a growing interest in sending humans to Mars and beyond. NASA has proposed the Artemis program, which aims to land the first woman and next man on the Moon by 2024, with the goal of establishing a sustainable human presence on the lunar surface by 2028. In addition, Elon Musk, the CEO of SpaceX, has proposed the Starship spacecraft, which is designed to transport humans and cargo to Mars and beyond.

To overcome the challenges of sending humans to Mars and beyond, significant advancements need to be made in several areas. These include developing more advanced propulsion systems that can transport humans to Mars in a shorter amount of time, as well as more efficient life support and waste management systems. In addition, new technologies, such as 3D printing and robotics, can be used to create self-sufficient habitats and infrastructure on Mars.

As space agencies and private companies continue to pursue missions to Mars and beyond, several technological and logistical challenges must be addressed to make these missions possible. One of the most significant challenges is the long-duration spaceflight required to travel to and from Mars, which can take anywhere from six to nine months each way. During this time, astronauts are exposed to various risks, including radiation exposure, muscle and bone atrophy, and psychological stress.

To address these risks, scientists and engineers are exploring new technologies and techniques to support long-duration spaceflight. One such technology is artificial gravity, which involves creating a rotating spacecraft that simulates Earth's gravity. Studies have shown that artificial gravity can help mitigate the effects of muscle and bone atrophy and reduce the risk of cardiovascular problems associated with extended periods of weightlessness.

Another critical challenge in space travel is the need for reliable and efficient life support systems. Astronauts must have access to food, water, and oxygen, and waste must be recycled and reused in closed-loop systems. To achieve this, researchers are developing advanced life support technologies that can sustain human life in space for extended periods. These technologies include closed-loop water recycling systems, advanced hydroponic farming techniques, and atmospheric processing systems.

In addition to technological challenges, space travel also poses several logistical challenges, including the need for reliable communication and navigation systems, advanced propulsion technologies, and the ability to land and launch from other planets. To address these challenges, space agencies and private companies are investing in research and development in various fields, including artificial intelligence, robotics, and materials science.

One area of particular interest is the development of new propulsion technologies that can reduce the travel time to Mars and other planets. Current chemical propulsion systems can take up to nine months to reach Mars, which presents significant risks and challenges for the crew. To address this challenge, researchers are exploring advanced propulsion systems such as nuclear propulsion, ion propulsion, and solar sails, which can significantly reduce travel time and make space exploration more efficient.

Finally, there is the challenge of providing astronauts with the resources they need to survive and thrive on other planets. This includes the need for habitats that can protect astronauts from radiation and extreme weather conditions, as well as the development of systems to mine and extract resources such as water and minerals from the planet's surface.

Despite these challenges, the future of space travel is exciting and holds great promise for humanity. With continued investment in research and development, it is possible to overcome these challenges and make human exploration of Mars and beyond a reality.

One of the most important considerations for long-duration space travel, such as a mission to Mars or beyond, is the psychological impact on the astronauts. Being confined in a small space for a long period of time, isolated from family and friends, and dealing with the stress of the mission itself can take a significant toll on the mental health of the crew. As such, it is essential to develop psychological support systems and methods for maintaining mental health during the journey.

One solution is to incorporate virtual reality technology into the spacecraft, allowing astronauts to "escape" into a simulated environment when needed. This technology can also be used to maintain connections with loved ones back on Earth, and to provide a sense of familiarity and comfort in an otherwise unfamiliar and isolated environment.

Another important consideration is the need for self-sufficiency during the mission. This includes developing sustainable food, water, and oxygen systems, as well as finding ways to repair or replace damaged equipment without the need for resupply missions. In order to achieve this, it will be necessary to develop technologies for regenerative life support systems, such as water recycling, and 3D printing for on-demand replacement parts.

There are also significant risks associated with long-duration space travel, such as radiation exposure, which can cause a range of health problems, including cancer and genetic mutations. To mitigate these risks, it will be necessary to develop new shielding technologies and medical treatments that can address the effects of long-term radiation exposure.

There are ethical and philosophical considerations related to the exploration of space. As humans expand into the cosmos, questions about ownership of celestial bodies, potential contamination of extraterrestrial environments, and the impact of space exploration on terrestrial ecosystems will need to be addressed. It will be important for scientists, policymakers, and the public to engage in ongoing discussions about these issues and to develop responsible frameworks for space exploration.

Another major challenge in space travel is the issue of radiation exposure. Cosmic radiation is a constant threat to the health of astronauts, and prolonged exposure to high levels of radiation can cause serious long-term health effects such as cancer and other diseases. NASA and other space agencies have been researching ways to mitigate this risk, such as developing advanced shielding materials and designing spacecraft with radiation-hardened components. However, more research is needed to fully understand the risks of radiation exposure and develop effective countermeasures.

In addition to the physical challenges of space travel, there are also numerous logistical and operational challenges that must be overcome. For example, the cost of space travel remains a major obstacle to the development of large-scale missions to Mars and beyond. The cost of building, launching, and maintaining a spacecraft capable of carrying humans and supplies to another planet is prohibitively expensive, and it will require significant investment from governments and private companies to make such missions a reality.

Furthermore, the distance and travel time involved in missions to Mars and other planets create additional logistical challenges. Even at their closest approach, Mars is still over 33 million miles away from Earth, and a round-trip mission could take up to two years to complete. This requires extensive planning and coordination to ensure that astronauts have the necessary supplies, equipment, and medical support to survive and operate effectively in the harsh environment of space.

Another important consideration is the need for sustainable and long-term support systems for human settlements on other planets. This includes developing systems for generating food, water, and oxygen, as well as providing adequate shelter and waste management capabilities. The success of any long-term human settlement on Mars or other planets will depend on the ability to establish self-sustaining systems that can support a growing population.

The success of space travel, especially in the context of human missions to other planets, hinges on a wide range of technological advancements. One of the most crucial areas of innovation that will facilitate long-duration human spaceflight is life support systems.

A life support system is a critical component of any space vehicle or habitat that will sustain human life in the harsh environment of space. The system is designed to provide the basic human necessities such as breathable air, clean water, and nutritious food. The system must also be able to manage waste and maintain a comfortable temperature and atmospheric pressure.

Traditional life support systems have been developed using conventional engineering approaches, but newer approaches based on bioregenerative life support systems (BLSS) show promise. BLSS uses biological systems, such as plants and algae, to convert waste into usable resources. These systems have the potential to reduce the amount of food, water, and oxygen that must be transported from Earth to space.

Another important area of innovation that will advance human missions to other planets is propulsion technology. Currently, most space missions use chemical rockets, which are highly inefficient and expensive. Electric propulsion, which uses ion engines or other forms of electric propulsion, is a promising alternative that could drastically reduce the cost of space travel.

The use of nuclear power and propulsion is also being explored. Nuclear thermal propulsion systems, which use nuclear reactions to heat a propellant and generate thrust, offer several advantages over chemical propulsion, including higher specific impulse and greater efficiency. Nuclear thermal propulsion could enable faster travel times and make long-duration missions to Mars and beyond more feasible.

In addition to these technological advancements, space travel will also require significant logistical innovations. The cost and complexity of sending humans to other planets will necessitate the development of in-situ resource utilization (ISRU) systems. These systems will allow astronauts to use resources found on the surface of the planet, such as water and minerals, to sustain themselves and support their mission.

The success of human missions to other planets will also require significant advances in the areas of autonomous robotics and artificial intelligence. Robotic systems will play a critical role in conducting exploratory missions and building infrastructure on other planets, while artificial intelligence will be used to help astronauts make critical decisions and navigate the complex environment of space.

As space agencies and private companies continue to work on developing the technologies required for long-duration spaceflight and establishing human settlements on other planets, several new challenges have emerged. One of the most significant challenges is the potential health risks posed by long-duration spaceflight.

Astronauts on the International Space Station (ISS) experience a number of health challenges related to the microgravity environment, including muscle and bone loss, cardiovascular changes, and vision problems. These changes are thought to be related to the effects of long-term exposure to microgravity, which is significantly different from the Earth's gravity. While scientists have developed exercise programs and other interventions to help mitigate these effects, there are concerns that these health risks could be much more severe on long-duration missions to Mars and beyond.

Another challenge is the psychological and social impact of long-duration spaceflight. Astronauts on the ISS are typically in space for six months at a time, but missions to Mars and other destinations could require crews to be in space for two to three years or more. This level of isolation and confinement could have significant psychological impacts, including depression, anxiety, and conflicts among crew members.

To address these challenges, scientists and engineers are exploring new technologies and strategies for long-duration spaceflight. One promising approach is the use of virtual reality (VR) to provide astronauts with immersive experiences that simulate Earth-like environments. VR technology could be used to create virtual landscapes, simulate social interactions, and provide other forms of stimulation that could help to alleviate the psychological impacts of long-duration spaceflight.

Another promising approach is the use of artificial intelligence (AI) and robotics to support human spaceflight. AI systems could be used to monitor crew health and wellbeing, as well as to manage spacecraft systems and support scientific research activities. Robotics could be used to assist with tasks such as maintenance and repairs, freeing up crew time for other activities.

In addition to these technological solutions, there is also a growing interest in exploring the social and cultural aspects of space travel. As humans begin to establish permanent settlements on other planets, it will be important to develop new social systems and cultural practices that can support long-term space living. This could include new forms of governance, new approaches to work and leisure, and new ways of thinking about identity and community.

One major challenge in space travel is the harsh and unforgiving nature of the space environment. Astronauts must cope with high levels of radiation, extreme temperatures, and the lack of a protective atmosphere. These challenges make it difficult for humans to live and work in space for extended periods of time.

One solution to this problem is to develop advanced spacesuits and habitats that can protect astronauts from the harsh space environment. Spacesuits must be durable and flexible enough to allow astronauts to move and work freely while protecting them from radiation and extreme temperatures. Habitats must provide a safe and comfortable living environment that can support human needs such as air, water, and food.

Another challenge of space travel is the long journey times and the need for advanced propulsion systems. Current chemical propulsion systems are not efficient enough for long-duration missions to other planets. For example, a typical mission to Mars takes about six to eight months using chemical propulsion. This long journey time can increase the risk to astronauts and decrease the feasibility of manned missions to other planets.

One potential solution is to develop new propulsion systems, such as nuclear thermal propulsion or antimatter propulsion, that are more efficient and can reduce travel times. These advanced propulsion systems could reduce the travel time to Mars to just a few weeks, making manned missions more feasible and reducing the risk to astronauts.

In addition to these technological challenges, there are also logistical and financial challenges to overcome in space travel. The cost of space missions is very high, and funding for space exploration is often limited. The development of new technologies and materials for space travel requires significant research and development efforts, which can be expensive and time-consuming.

To overcome these challenges, international cooperation and partnerships may be necessary to share resources and knowledge. Private companies and commercial ventures may also play an important role in advancing space travel technology and making it more accessible.

While technological advances have enabled humans to venture beyond our own planet, space travel remains a challenging and risky endeavor. To achieve the goal of sending humans to Mars and beyond, there are a number of technological and logistical challenges that must be addressed.

One of the primary challenges is the development of more advanced propulsion systems. Current rocket technology is limited in its ability to carry large payloads over long distances, and the time required for travel to deep space destinations is also a significant obstacle. In order to overcome these limitations, there is a need for the development of advanced propulsion systems that are both more efficient and faster.

Another challenge is the development of new life support systems that are capable of sustaining human life for extended periods in space. These systems must be able to provide food, water, and oxygen, while also removing waste and maintaining an appropriate atmospheric composition. Additionally, the effects of long-term exposure to radiation and microgravity must also be addressed.

Logistical challenges also exist in terms of the necessary infrastructure required to support human space travel. The development of more advanced spacecraft capable of carrying larger payloads is critical, as is the construction of space habitats that can serve as bases for humans during extended missions. In addition, the establishment of supply chains and transportation systems for materials and equipment will be necessary to sustain operations over the long term.

Another critical aspect of space travel is the human element. Human psychology and physiology must be considered in the design of future space missions. Strategies for maintaining crew morale and addressing potential psychological stressors must be developed, as well as methods for addressing medical emergencies and other health issues that may arise during space travel.

The cost remains a significant barrier to the development of advanced space travel technologies. While private companies such as SpaceX and Blue Origin have made strides in reducing the cost of spaceflight, the cost of developing and maintaining advanced technologies remains high. To overcome this challenge, partnerships between private industry and government agencies, as well as international collaboration, may be necessary.

One of the major challenges of human space travel is radiation exposure. During long-duration space missions, astronauts are exposed to a significant amount of radiation, which can have serious health implications. Radiation exposure can increase the risk of cancer, damage the central nervous system, and impair cognitive function. Shielding spacecraft from radiation is a major challenge, as some types of radiation, such as high-energy particles, are difficult to block with traditional materials.

Researchers are exploring a variety of strategies to mitigate the risks of radiation exposure during space travel. One approach is to develop new radiation shielding materials that are more effective at blocking harmful radiation. For example, researchers at NASA have been exploring the use of high-density polyethylene (HDPE) as a radiation shield. HDPE is a lightweight, durable plastic that can be easily molded into different shapes, making it a versatile material for spacecraft design. In lab tests, HDPE has been shown to be effective at blocking high-energy protons and other types of radiation.

Another strategy for mitigating radiation exposure during space travel is to develop medical countermeasures that can protect astronauts from the harmful effects of radiation. For example, researchers are exploring the use of antioxidants, such as vitamin E and melatonin, which have been shown to reduce oxidative stress and DNA damage caused by radiation exposure. Other potential countermeasures include drugs that can stimulate the body's natural repair mechanisms, as well as vaccines that can enhance the immune system's ability to fight off radiation-induced cancer.

In addition to radiation exposure, space travel poses a variety of other challenges, including microgravity, isolation, and psychological stress. Microgravity can lead to a loss of bone density and muscle mass, as well as changes in vision and cardiovascular function. Isolation and confinement can have negative psychological effects, such as depression and anxiety, and can impair cognitive function. To overcome these challenges, researchers are exploring a variety of approaches, such as exercise regimens, dietary interventions, and virtual reality technologies.

One promising approach for mitigating the effects of microgravity is exercise. Researchers have found that regular exercise can help prevent the loss of bone density and muscle mass, as well as improve cardiovascular function. In addition, exercise has been shown to have positive effects on mood and cognitive function, which can help mitigate the psychological effects of isolation and confinement. To this end, NASA has developed a variety of exercise equipment for use on spacecraft, including treadmills, stationary bikes, and resistance bands.

Another potential solution for mitigating the psychological effects of isolation and confinement is virtual reality (VR) technology. VR can provide astronauts with a sense of immersion and connection to the outside world, which can help reduce feelings of isolation and depression. In addition, VR has been shown to have positive effects on cognitive function, such as memory and attention. To this end, NASA has developed a variety of VR applications for use on spacecraft, including simulations of Earth and other planets, as well as immersive training programs for astronauts.

There are several technological and logistical challenges that must be overcome before human missions to Mars and beyond can become a reality. One of the biggest challenges is the development of propulsion systems that can efficiently and safely transport large payloads over long distances in space. While traditional chemical rockets have been used to launch spacecraft into space for decades, they are not well-suited for long-duration missions to other planets because they require enormous amounts of fuel, which adds significant weight to the spacecraft and makes it more difficult to reach high speeds.

One proposed solution to this challenge is the development of advanced propulsion systems, such as nuclear thermal propulsion (NTP) and electric propulsion (EP), that can provide greater thrust and efficiency than chemical rockets. NTP involves using a nuclear reactor to heat a propellant, such as liquid hydrogen, which is then expelled through a nozzle to generate thrust. EP systems, on the other hand, use electric fields or magnetic fields to accelerate charged particles, such as ions, to high speeds, which can generate significant thrust with a much lower fuel mass.

Another major challenge of human space travel is the need to create and sustain a habitable environment for astronauts in deep space. This includes providing adequate food, water, and breathable air, as well as protecting astronauts from the harsh radiation and extreme temperatures of space. To address these challenges, researchers are developing new technologies for recycling water, generating oxygen, and producing food in space, as well as creating more advanced radiation shielding materials.

Additionally, the psychological and social effects of long-duration space travel on astronauts must also be considered. The isolation and confinement of spaceflight can lead to negative psychological effects, such as depression, anxiety, and interpersonal conflict. To mitigate these risks, space agencies are developing training programs to help astronauts cope with the challenges of spaceflight, as well as designing spacecraft and habitats that provide adequate living space and opportunities for social interaction.

Another major challenge of human space travel is the high cost associated with developing and launching spacecraft, which can limit the number and scope of missions that can be undertaken. To address this challenge, space agencies and private companies are exploring new models for space exploration, such as public-private partnerships and international collaboration. These models can help reduce costs by sharing resources and expertise, as well as allowing for more ambitious missions that would be difficult to undertake by a single organization.

One of the major technological and logistical challenges of space travel is the issue of radiation exposure. As humans travel further into space, they are exposed to high levels of radiation from cosmic rays and solar flares. These particles can cause serious health problems, such as cancer, cardiovascular disease, and damage to the nervous system.

To address this challenge, researchers are developing advanced shielding materials to protect astronauts from radiation exposure. For example, scientists are exploring the use of water as a radiation shield, as it is a highly effective absorber of high-energy radiation. Water can be used as a shield on the walls of a spacecraft, as well as in a water-filled spacesuit. In addition, materials such as polyethylene, which is used in some types of plastic, have been found to be effective radiation shields.

Another approach to reducing radiation exposure is to develop pharmaceutical countermeasures that can protect astronauts from the harmful effects of radiation. For example, studies have shown that certain drugs, such as melatonin and amifostine, can protect against radiation damage to DNA and reduce the risk of cancer.

In addition to the challenges of radiation exposure, there are also technological challenges associated with space travel. One of the most important challenges is the development of more efficient propulsion systems. Current spacecraft propulsion systems, such as chemical rockets, are limited in terms of speed and range. To travel further into space, researchers are exploring new propulsion technologies, such as nuclear rockets and ion drives.

Nuclear rockets use the energy from nuclear reactions to heat a propellant and create thrust. This technology has the potential to significantly reduce travel times and increase the range of spacecraft. However, it also presents significant safety and environmental challenges, as well as political and regulatory hurdles.

Ion drives, on the other hand, use electric fields to accelerate ions and create thrust. This technology is more efficient than chemical rockets and has already been used in some space missions, such as the Dawn spacecraft that explored the asteroid belt. However, ion drives are still limited in terms of their thrust and speed capabilities, and further research is needed to develop more advanced versions of this technology.

Other technological challenges associated with space travel include the development of advanced life support systems, such as closed-loop systems that can recycle air, water, and waste. This will be essential for long-duration space missions, such as a mission to Mars. In addition, researchers are exploring the use of 3D printing and other advanced manufacturing techniques to produce spare parts and other equipment in space, reducing the need for resupply missions from Earth.

One of the biggest challenges of space travel is the high cost associated with it. Even with the development of reusable rockets, the cost of transporting humans and supplies to Mars and beyond will still be significant. As such, finding ways to reduce the cost of space travel will be a critical factor in the future of space exploration.

One potential solution to reducing the cost of space travel is through the use of space mining. There are potentially vast reserves of valuable resources, such as water, metals, and minerals, on other planets and asteroids that could be mined and used to support human colonies. For example, water can be used for drinking, irrigation, and the production of rocket fuel. The use of space mining would not only reduce the cost of transporting materials from Earth, but it could also lead to the development of new industries and economic opportunities.

Another challenge of space travel is the exposure of humans to radiation. Radiation exposure can lead to long-term health effects, including an increased risk of cancer, and it can also impact the performance of electronic equipment. To overcome this challenge, new materials and technologies will need to be developed to protect humans and equipment from the effects of radiation. This could involve the use of radiation-shielding materials, such as lead or polyethylene, or the development of new electronic components that are more resistant to radiation.

One of the key technological challenges of sending humans to Mars and beyond is the development of sustainable life support systems. On Earth, we have access to the resources necessary to sustain human life, such as air, water, and food. However, on other planets, we will need to develop closed-loop systems that can sustain human life for extended periods. This will require the development of technologies such as advanced water recycling systems, greenhouse technologies for growing food, and energy systems that are capable of generating power in a sustainable way.

One of the most significant challenges in long-duration space travel is the issue of radiation exposure. When astronauts venture beyond the protection of the Earth's magnetic field, they become vulnerable to the constant bombardment of ionizing radiation from cosmic rays and solar storms. These high-energy particles can damage cells, disrupt biological processes, and increase the risk of cancer and other diseases.

To mitigate the risks of radiation exposure, several strategies are being explored. One approach is to develop better shielding materials that can provide effective protection against cosmic radiation. Researchers are investigating new materials such as aerogels, boron nitride nanotubes, and composite structures that can offer greater protection while being lightweight and easy to transport.

Another strategy is to develop countermeasures that can enhance the body's natural defenses against radiation. For example, some studies have shown that the antioxidant properties of certain compounds, such as resveratrol, can help mitigate the damage caused by radiation. Other research has focused on using gene therapy to enhance the expression of specific genes that can repair DNA damage and reduce the risk of cancer.

In addition to radiation, long-duration space missions present a host of other challenges, including the physical and psychological effects of microgravity, the limited availability of resources such as food and water, and the need for reliable life support systems. To address these challenges, NASA and other space agencies are investing in a range of technologies and strategies, including:

Advanced life support systems that can generate food, water, and oxygen from waste materials and other sources, reducing the need for resupply missions.

Novel propulsion technologies that can enable faster and more efficient travel, such as nuclear thermal propulsion and fusion-based propulsion.

Smart habitats and living spaces that can adapt to the changing needs of the crew and provide a comfortable and healthy environment for long-duration missions.

Advanced robotics and autonomous systems that can perform tasks and maintenance activities, reducing the workload for crew members and enabling them to focus on high-priority tasks.

While the challenges of long-duration space travel are significant, the rewards of space exploration and colonization are equally great. By venturing beyond the confines of our home planet, we can gain a better understanding of the universe and our place in it. We can explore new frontiers, discover new resources, and push the boundaries of human knowledge and achievement. With the continued development of new technologies and approaches, the future of space travel is full of promise and potential.

In addition to the scientific and technological advancements necessary for successful space travel, there are also social and ethical considerations that need to be addressed. One major issue is the potential impact on human health during long-duration space missions. Astronauts on extended missions will be exposed to higher levels of radiation and microgravity, which can cause a range of health problems, including bone loss, muscle atrophy, cardiovascular problems, and cognitive decline. Developing effective countermeasures to these issues will be critical to ensure the health and safety of future space travelers.

Another challenge is the psychological impact of long-duration space travel. Spending months or even years in a confined, isolated environment can take a toll on astronauts' mental health, leading to depression, anxiety, and other psychological issues. Addressing these issues will be critical to ensure the well-being of space travelers and to maintain their effectiveness in carrying out mission objectives.

There are also ethical concerns surrounding space travel, particularly with regard to the potential for contamination of other planets and celestial bodies. If humans are not careful, they could inadvertently introduce Earth-based life forms to other planets, potentially disrupting or even destroying existing ecosystems. Careful planning and adherence to established protocols for preventing contamination will be necessary to ensure that the search for extraterrestrial life does not inadvertently harm other worlds.

There are also social and economic implications of space travel. Space exploration is an expensive endeavor, and the resources required for space travel could be put to use in other areas, such as improving healthcare, education, and infrastructure on Earth. At the same time, however, space travel has the potential to inspire and unite people around the world, fostering a sense of shared purpose and encouraging scientific and technological innovation.

As space travel advances, there is also the issue of funding. Space exploration and colonization requires massive amounts of funding and investment, and without it, progress could be significantly delayed. Governments have been the primary source of funding for space exploration in the past, but with the emergence of private companies, the funding landscape is changing.

Private space companies such as SpaceX, Blue Origin, and Virgin Galactic are investing in space exploration and offering new opportunities for private individuals to invest. The growing private space sector has sparked new innovations in space travel, with companies like SpaceX developing reusable rockets and spacecraft that are more cost-effective and efficient than traditional space technology.

Another major technological challenge for space travel is the development of new propulsion systems. Currently, most space missions rely on chemical propulsion systems, which are limited in their capabilities and require significant amounts of fuel. New propulsion technologies, such as nuclear thermal propulsion and plasma-based systems, offer the potential for faster and more efficient space travel.

There are also significant logistical challenges to overcome in order to send humans to Mars and beyond. One of the biggest challenges is maintaining a steady supply of resources, such as food, water, and air, for the duration of the mission. NASA and other space agencies are working on developing sustainable life support systems and technologies to help astronauts survive for extended periods of time in space.

Additionally, long-term exposure to space radiation poses a significant risk to human health. Radiation can cause a range of health problems, including cancer, cardiovascular disease, and neurological damage. Developing effective radiation shielding technologies is crucial for protecting astronauts during long-duration space missions.

In conclusion, the future of space travel holds tremendous promise, and there are many technological and logistical challenges to overcome. However, with continued investment, collaboration, and innovation, we can make significant progress in our efforts to send humans to Mars and beyond. The development of new propulsion technologies, advanced life support systems, and efficient in situ resource utilization techniques will be essential in enabling long-duration space missions. In addition, international cooperation and public-private partnerships will be critical in advancing our understanding of the universe and achieving our goals in space exploration. By leveraging the collective expertise and resources of the global community, we can take bold steps forward in expanding human presence in the solar system and unlocking the secrets of the cosmos.

CHAPTER VII

How can we harness the power of quantum computing to solve complex problems in fields such as chemistry and materials science?

Introduction:

Quantum computing is a rapidly developing field that holds immense potential for solving complex problems that are beyond the reach of classical computers. Quantum computers operate on the principles of quantum mechanics, allowing for parallel computation and the ability to perform complex calculations much faster than classical computers. One promising application of quantum computing is in the fields of chemistry and materials science, where it can be used to model and design new materials, and to solve complex chemical problems. This paper explores how quantum computing can be harnessed to address the challenges of chemistry and materials science, and the potential impact of this technology.

Body:

The challenges of chemistry and materials science

Chemistry and materials science are two fields that are critical to the advancement of technology, but also present significant challenges. The development of new materials, for instance, requires a deep understanding of the underlying chemistry, as well as the ability to model and simulate the behavior of materials at the molecular level. This can be a time-consuming and resource-intensive process, particularly for complex materials with many interacting components.

The potential of quantum computing

Quantum computing holds great promise for addressing the challenges of chemistry and materials science. Because quantum computers operate on the principles of quantum mechanics, they can simulate the behavior of molecules and materials much more efficiently than classical computers. This can lead to significant advances in the design of new materials, the discovery of new chemical reactions, and the development of more efficient energy sources.

Examples of quantum computing in action

There have already been several successful applications of quantum computing in the fields of chemistry and materials science. For example, researchers at IBM used a quantum computer to simulate the behavior of beryllium hydride, a molecule with six electrons. The simulation would have taken a classical computer 10,000 years to complete, but the quantum computer was able to do it in just a few minutes. This breakthrough demonstrates the potential for quantum computing to revolutionize the field of materials science.

Challenges to quantum computing

While quantum computing has the potential to transform the field of chemistry and materials science, there are also significant challenges that must be overcome. One major challenge is the issue of qubit stability. Quantum computers rely on qubits, which are highly sensitive to their environment and can easily become disrupted. As a result, quantum computers must be operated in highly controlled environments, making them expensive and difficult to maintain.

Future directions and impact

Despite these challenges, the potential impact of quantum computing on chemistry and materials science is significant. With continued advances in technology, quantum computers have the potential to revolutionize the field, leading to the development of new materials, more efficient energy sources, and a better understanding of the fundamental principles of chemistry. This could have a profound impact on fields such as energy, medicine, and materials science, leading to new discoveries and advances that were previously thought impossible.

As quantum computing continues to develop, the potential for its application in solving complex problems in fields such as chemistry and materials science becomes increasingly evident. One area in which quantum computing shows great promise is in the simulation of quantum systems. Simulating these systems is essential for understanding chemical and material processes, but classical computers struggle to accurately model them due to their complexity.

Quantum computing, on the other hand, is uniquely suited to simulating quantum systems. One of the main reasons for this is the phenomenon of quantum entanglement, which allows multiple qubits (the basic unit of quantum computing) to be connected in such a way that the state of one qubit is dependent on the state of the others. This allows quantum computers to perform calculations that would be impossible for classical computers.

In the field of chemistry, quantum computing can be used to simulate the behavior of molecules and their interactions. This has numerous practical applications, including drug discovery, materials science, and the design of new catalysts. By accurately modeling these systems, researchers can predict how they will behave under different conditions, enabling the development of new drugs and materials that would be difficult or impossible to discover through traditional experimentation.

Similarly, in materials science, quantum computing can be used to simulate the behavior of materials at the atomic and molecular level, providing insights into their physical properties, electronic structure, and behavior under different conditions. This could lead to the development of new materials with novel properties, such as improved strength, increased conductivity, or enhanced catalytic activity.

Another potential application of quantum computing in chemistry and materials science is the optimization of chemical reactions. By modeling the behavior of reactants and products at the molecular level, researchers can identify the most efficient pathways for chemical reactions, leading to the development of more effective and sustainable manufacturing processes.

In addition to its applications in simulating quantum systems, quantum computing can also be used to solve complex optimization problems. One example of this is the traveling salesman problem, which involves finding the shortest possible route between a set of cities. While this may seem like a simple problem, it becomes incredibly complex as the number of cities increases. Classical computers struggle to solve this problem efficiently, but quantum computers have the potential to do so in a fraction of the time.

There are, however, significant challenges to harnessing the power of quantum computing. One major issue is the high error rate of quantum systems, which can lead to inaccuracies in calculations. Researchers are actively working on developing error-correcting algorithms and other methods to mitigate this problem, but it remains a significant hurdle to the practical application of quantum computing.

Another challenge is the high cost of building and maintaining quantum computers. The technology is still in its infancy, and quantum computers remain prohibitively expensive for all but the most well-funded research institutions and corporations. This means that many researchers in the field of chemistry and materials science may not have access to the technology needed to harness its power.

Quantum computing is still in its early stages of development, and many researchers believe that it has the potential to revolutionize a variety of fields, including chemistry and materials science. One of the primary advantages of quantum computing is its ability to solve complex problems much more quickly than classical computers.

In the field of chemistry, one of the most promising applications of quantum computing is in the simulation of molecular systems. Quantum computers can calculate the energy states and interactions of molecules with much greater accuracy and speed than classical computers, which is particularly important in the design of new drugs and materials. For example, quantum computing could be used to accurately model the behavior of proteins in the body, leading to the development of new drugs that are more effective and have fewer side effects.

In materials science, quantum computing could be used to simulate the behavior of materials at the atomic level, which is critical for understanding the properties of new materials and developing advanced manufacturing techniques. For example, researchers could use quantum computers to simulate the behavior of superconducting materials, which could lead to the development of new technologies such as quantum computers and energy storage devices.

Another area where quantum computing could have a significant impact is in cryptography. Quantum computers are able to perform certain types of calculations much more quickly than classical computers, which could make some forms of encryption vulnerable to attack. However, quantum computing could also be used to develop new encryption methods that are much more secure than current techniques.

Despite the many potential applications of quantum computing, there are still significant technical and logistical challenges that must be overcome before it becomes a practical tool for solving complex problems in fields such as chemistry and materials science. One of the primary challenges is the issue of quantum decoherence, which occurs when quantum systems lose their coherence due to interactions with the environment. To overcome this challenge, researchers are developing techniques for error correction and fault tolerance that could make quantum computers much more reliable and practical for real-world applications.

In addition, quantum computers are still relatively expensive and difficult to build and operate. While progress is being made in developing new hardware and software for quantum computing, it will likely be many years before quantum computers are widely available and affordable enough to be used in research and development.

Quantum computing has the potential to revolutionize many areas of science, from computational chemistry and materials science to cryptography and optimization. By exploiting the properties of quantum mechanics, quantum computers can solve certain problems exponentially faster than classical computers. This makes them particularly well-suited for tasks that require massive amounts of computational power, such as simulating complex chemical reactions or optimizing complex systems.

One of the most promising applications of quantum computing is in the field of computational chemistry. Quantum computers can simulate the behavior of atoms and molecules with unprecedented accuracy and speed, allowing researchers to understand complex chemical reactions and design new molecules with desired properties. This has enormous implications for drug discovery, as researchers can use quantum computers to simulate the interactions between drugs and their targets, predicting which compounds are most likely to be effective and minimizing the need for expensive and time-consuming experiments.

Another field that stands to benefit from quantum computing is materials science. Quantum computers can simulate the behavior of electrons in materials, allowing researchers to design new materials with specific properties. This could lead to the development of new materials for use in everything from high-performance electronics to energy storage devices.

However, there are also significant challenges to be overcome before quantum computers can be widely used in these and other fields. One major challenge is the issue of quantum error correction. Because quantum systems are inherently fragile and subject to noise and other forms of interference, maintaining the coherence of qubits over long periods of time is extremely difficult. This means that quantum computers must be designed with error-correcting mechanisms that can detect and correct errors in the qubits.

Another challenge is the difficulty of scaling up quantum computers to handle larger and more complex problems. While small-scale quantum computers have been developed and demonstrated in the laboratory, building a quantum computer with thousands or millions of qubits is still a daunting task. This requires not only advances in hardware technology, but also new algorithms and software tools that can take advantage of the power of quantum computing.

Despite these challenges, many researchers and organizations are working to harness the power of quantum computing for a wide range of applications. In addition to academic research programs, companies such as IBM, Google, and Microsoft are investing heavily in quantum computing research and development. Governments around the world are also recognizing the potential of quantum computing, with initiatives such as the US National Quantum Initiative and the European Union's Quantum Flagship program providing funding and support for research and development.

In the coming years, it is likely that quantum computing will continue to play an increasingly important role in many areas of science and technology. While there are still significant technical challenges to be overcome, the potential benefits of quantum computing are too great to be ignored. As researchers continue to push the boundaries of what is possible with quantum computing, we may see the development of entirely new fields of science and technology, as well as the transformation of existing fields.

Quantum computing can offer an opportunity to solve some of the biggest challenges faced by science and technology today. While classical computing uses bits that can represent either 0 or 1, quantum computing employs quantum bits, or qubits, that can represent both 0 and 1 at the same time. This means that quantum computers can perform certain calculations much faster than classical computers.

One area where quantum computing can have a significant impact is in the field of chemistry. Chemistry involves understanding the properties and behavior of molecules and reactions, which are often complex and difficult to simulate. Quantum computing can help us better understand the electronic structures and reactions of molecules, allowing for more efficient drug design and discovery, as well as the development of new materials.

Quantum computers can also help to overcome challenges in materials science. Materials science involves understanding the properties and behavior of materials, and developing new materials with specific properties for various applications. However, simulating the behavior of materials at the atomic and molecular scale can be incredibly challenging for classical computers. With quantum computing, it may be possible to simulate the behavior of materials at this scale much more efficiently, leading to the development of new materials with novel properties.

Another area where quantum computing can have an impact is in optimization problems. These are problems where the goal is to find the best solution among a large number of possibilities. For example, in logistics, the traveling salesman problem involves finding the shortest route that visits a given set of cities. This is a notoriously difficult problem to solve using classical computing, but quantum computing could offer a much faster solution.

Furthermore, quantum computing can also help to improve cybersecurity. One of the most well-known applications of quantum computing is its potential to break cryptographic codes that are currently in use. However, it can also help to develop new cryptographic methods that are more secure, using quantum encryption to transmit information securely.

One of the most promising applications of quantum computing is in the field of chemistry, where it has the potential to revolutionize the way we design and discover new materials. Quantum computing can solve problems that are intractable for classical computers, which makes it well-suited for simulating the behavior of atoms and molecules in complex chemical reactions. This could lead to the development of new drugs and materials that are more effective and efficient than anything currently available.

One area where quantum computing could have a significant impact is in the development of new catalysts for chemical reactions. Catalysts are substances that accelerate chemical reactions without being consumed in the process, and they are essential for many industrial processes, such as the production of fuels and plastics. However, designing new catalysts is a time-consuming and expensive process that requires a great deal of trial and error. With quantum computing, researchers can simulate the behavior of potential catalysts and predict which ones are most likely to be effective, reducing the time and cost of the development process.

Another area where quantum computing could be transformative is in the study of superconductors, which are materials that conduct electricity with zero resistance at extremely low temperatures. Superconductors have the potential to revolutionize many industries, from power generation and transmission to transportation and computing. However, their behavior is still poorly understood, which limits their potential applications. Quantum computing can help to simulate the behavior of superconductors and identify new materials that exhibit this property at higher temperatures, which could make them more practical for everyday use.

In addition to chemistry and materials science, quantum computing is also being explored for use in other fields such as finance, logistics, and cryptography. For example, quantum computers can be used to solve complex optimization problems that arise in logistics and supply chain management. They can also be used to break certain types of encryption, which has important implications for data security and privacy.

While quantum computing is still in its early stages, it has the potential to revolutionize the way we approach many complex problems in fields such as chemistry and materials science. As quantum computing technology continues to evolve, we can expect to see more breakthroughs in these areas that will have important implications for our lives and the world around us.

One of the major fields where quantum computing has shown immense potential is in the study of chemical reactions. Chemical reactions are difficult to simulate on classical computers because they involve the interaction of numerous particles, each of which has to be modeled separately. With quantum computing, however, the vast number of interactions between particles can be modeled simultaneously, making it possible to simulate chemical reactions more accurately and at a much faster rate.

In fact, quantum computing has already been used to solve problems in the field of chemistry. For example, researchers have used quantum computing to simulate the behavior of small molecules and predict their properties, such as bond energies, electronic structures, and reaction rates. This has the potential to greatly accelerate the process of drug discovery, as it allows researchers to simulate the interactions between potential drug compounds and biological molecules and predict their efficacy.

Quantum computing has also shown promise in the field of materials science. Materials science involves the study of the physical and chemical properties of materials and how they can be manipulated to create new materials with desired properties. One of the major challenges in materials science is the prediction of the properties of new materials before they are actually synthesized. This process is currently time-consuming and expensive, as it involves trial-and-error experimentation.

With quantum computing, however, it may be possible to accurately predict the properties of new materials without the need for extensive experimentation. For example, researchers have used quantum computing to predict the electronic properties of graphene, a material made up of a single layer of carbon atoms. These predictions were later confirmed through experimental measurements, indicating the accuracy of the quantum computing approach.

Another area where quantum computing has the potential to make a significant impact is in the field of cryptography. Classical cryptography is based on the idea of using mathematical algorithms to encode and decode messages. However, as computing power has increased, these algorithms have become easier to crack. Quantum cryptography, on the other hand, is based on the principles of quantum mechanics and involves the use of quantum bits, or qubits, to encode and transmit information. Because of the way qubits behave, it is extremely difficult for an eavesdropper to intercept the message without altering it in a way that is detectable by the sender and receiver.

However, while quantum computing holds great promise, there are still significant challenges that need to be overcome before it can be fully realized. One of the major challenges is the issue of qubit stability. Qubits are highly sensitive to their environment, and even minor disruptions can cause them to lose their quantum properties. This makes it difficult to build a stable and reliable quantum computer.

Another challenge is the issue of scalability. While quantum computing has shown promise in solving small-scale problems, it remains unclear whether it will be possible to scale up to solve larger and more complex problems. In addition, the development of quantum algorithms is still in its early stages, and it remains to be seen whether quantum computing will be able to outperform classical computing for a wide range of applications.

Quantum computing can also have a significant impact on the development of new materials. The discovery of new materials with improved properties is crucial to developing new technologies. Classical computers are limited in their ability to simulate the behavior of molecules and materials, which is necessary to understand their properties and optimize their performance. This is where quantum computers can make a significant contribution.

By simulating the behavior of molecules and materials, quantum computers can help accelerate the discovery of new materials with desirable properties. For example, they can be used to simulate the behavior of complex materials such as high-temperature superconductors or new battery materials. This can lead to the discovery of materials with improved properties, such as higher energy storage capacity or better conductivity.

One example of how quantum computing is already being used in materials science is in the development of new catalysts. Catalysts are substances that accelerate chemical reactions, and they are widely used in industrial processes. However, the development of new catalysts is a complex and time-consuming process. Quantum computers can be used to simulate the behavior of different catalysts, which can help identify the most promising candidates for further study.

In addition to materials science and chemistry, quantum computing has the potential to revolutionize many other fields. For example, it can be used to optimize logistics and transportation, improve weather forecasting, and enhance machine learning algorithms. As quantum computers become more powerful and more widely available, we can expect to see even more breakthroughs in a wide range of fields.

However, there are still many challenges that need to be overcome before quantum computing can reach its full potential. One major challenge is the issue of error correction. Quantum computers are highly sensitive to errors, which can quickly accumulate and cause the computation to fail. Researchers are working on developing error correction techniques that can address this problem, but this remains a significant challenge.

Another challenge is the limited availability of quantum computers. At present, quantum computers are expensive and difficult to build and maintain. This limits the number of researchers who have access to these machines, which in turn limits the rate of progress in the field. However, this situation is expected to improve as more companies and research institutions invest in the development of quantum computing technology.

Quantum computing has the potential to transform many fields beyond chemistry and materials science. For example, it can be used in cryptography, finance, logistics, and many other areas. As more research is conducted in this field, the potential applications for quantum computing are only increasing.

One of the main challenges with quantum computing is the issue of stability and coherence. Quantum systems are sensitive to external factors such as temperature, electromagnetic radiation, and magnetic fields, which can cause errors and limit the effectiveness of the system. This challenge has led researchers to explore different approaches to stabilize quantum systems, including the use of error correction codes and quantum error correction techniques.

Another challenge is the high cost and technical complexity of building quantum computers. The current state of quantum computing technology is still relatively experimental, and the practical applications of quantum computing are still in the development stage. However, with continued research and development, it is expected that the cost and complexity of building quantum computers will decrease over time, making it more accessible to businesses and researchers.

In addition to these challenges, there are also ethical considerations surrounding the use of quantum computing, especially in fields such as cryptography. As quantum computers become more powerful, they could potentially break existing encryption methods, which could have significant consequences for privacy and security. This has led to increased interest in developing post-quantum encryption methods that are resistant to quantum computing attacks.

Quantum computing has emerged as a promising technology that can potentially revolutionize various fields of science and engineering. It has the potential to solve complex problems that are beyond the capability of classical computers. In chemistry and materials science, quantum computing is seen as a powerful tool to solve many of the unsolved problems. One of the major problems in these fields is the determination of the properties of complex molecules and materials. The classical computers lack the capacity to deal with the enormous amount of data and calculations required to solve these problems. However, quantum computers are capable of solving these problems in a fraction of the time that classical computers would require.

One of the key advantages of quantum computing is its ability to perform parallel computations. Quantum computing utilizes qubits, which are analogous to classical bits but with the capability of existing in multiple states simultaneously. This ability allows quantum computers to perform parallel computations, which enables them to process large datasets in much less time than classical computers. In the field of chemistry and materials science, quantum computers can simulate the behavior of molecules and materials in parallel, which is essential for solving complex problems. Quantum computers can be used to simulate chemical reactions, which would be useful for designing new drugs and materials.

Quantum computers can also help solve the problem of energy storage, which is one of the biggest challenges in the renewable energy sector. Renewable energy sources such as solar and wind are variable in nature, and therefore, there is a need for efficient energy storage systems to ensure the stability of the grid. Quantum computers can be used to design new materials for energy storage, such as batteries and superconductors. Quantum computers can also simulate the behavior of molecules involved in energy storage, which is useful for understanding the processes involved in energy storage and for developing more efficient energy storage systems.

One of the challenges in harnessing the power of quantum computing is the need for error correction. Quantum systems are susceptible to noise, which can result in errors in calculations. Therefore, quantum computers require error correction to ensure the accuracy of the results. Several error-correcting codes have been developed, such as the surface code and the color code. These codes are used to detect and correct errors in quantum computations.

Another challenge in harnessing the power of quantum computing is the need for specialized hardware. Quantum computers require specialized hardware, which includes cryogenic cooling, precise control of the environment, and specialized components such as qubits and gates. However, with the recent advancements in quantum hardware, this challenge is being addressed. Many tech companies such as IBM, Google, and Microsoft have developed quantum computers that are accessible through cloud computing, making quantum computing more accessible to researchers and scientists.

Quantum computing has the potential to revolutionize many fields, including chemistry and materials science. In these fields, quantum computing could help in the design and discovery of new materials and drugs, as well as in the understanding of chemical reactions.

One area where quantum computing can have a significant impact is in the simulation of chemical reactions. The simulation of chemical reactions is a complex problem that can be computationally expensive, even for the most powerful classical computers. Quantum computing, on the other hand, has the potential to solve this problem more efficiently.

Quantum computing can also be used to simulate the behavior of materials at the atomic level. This can be useful in the design and discovery of new materials with specific properties. For example, a material with high conductivity could be used in the development of faster and more efficient electronic devices.

Another area where quantum computing could be useful is in the design of new drugs. The discovery of new drugs is a complex and time-consuming process that involves the screening of millions of potential candidates. Quantum computing could help in the screening of potential candidates by simulating the interactions between drugs and their targets.

In addition to its potential applications in chemistry and materials science, quantum computing can also have a significant impact on fields such as finance, cryptography, and machine learning. The ability of quantum computers to perform complex calculations more efficiently than classical computers can lead to the development of new algorithms and computational methods that could improve the accuracy and speed of many processes.

Despite the many potential applications of quantum computing, there are still several challenges that need to be overcome before it can become a practical tool for solving real-world problems. One of the biggest challenges is the issue of noise and errors. Quantum systems are sensitive to external disturbances, which can lead to errors in the computation. Researchers are currently developing new methods to mitigate these errors, including error-correction codes and fault-tolerant quantum computing.

Another challenge is the lack of commercially available quantum hardware. Although there have been significant advances in the development of quantum hardware in recent years, the technology is still in its early stages, and the cost of building and maintaining quantum computers is high.

Furthermore, the development of new quantum algorithms and computational methods is also necessary to fully realize the potential of quantum computing. This requires collaboration between quantum computing researchers and experts in various fields to identify the most pressing problems and develop innovative solutions.

Quantum computing is still a developing field and it is currently being used to solve complex problems in various industries. In the field of chemistry, quantum computing has the potential to transform the way we approach molecular simulations and drug discovery. The complex nature of molecular interactions makes it difficult to simulate using traditional computers, but quantum computers can provide much more accurate simulations that can help researchers develop new drugs and materials.

Quantum computing can also be used in materials science to help researchers design new materials with specific properties. Materials science is concerned with the discovery, design, and development of new materials that have desired properties, such as improved strength, durability, and conductivity. With the power of quantum computing, researchers can explore a much larger design space and identify materials with properties that were previously unknown.

One of the biggest challenges in harnessing the power of quantum computing is the development of algorithms that can take advantage of the unique properties of quantum systems. Traditional algorithms are not designed to run on quantum computers, so researchers are developing new algorithms that can take advantage of the specific capabilities of quantum systems, such as superposition and entanglement. Once these algorithms are developed, they can be used to solve complex problems in fields such as chemistry and materials science.

In addition to developing new algorithms, researchers are also working on improving the hardware used in quantum computing. One of the biggest challenges in quantum computing is maintaining the delicate quantum states that are required for calculations. Any external interference or noise can cause the system to collapse, making it difficult to achieve accurate results. To address this challenge, researchers are developing new technologies that can better isolate quantum systems from external interference and improve the stability of quantum states.

Another challenge in quantum computing is scaling the technology to a level where it can be used for practical applications. Currently, most quantum computers are still relatively small and can only perform a limited number of calculations. However, as the technology continues to improve, it is expected that quantum computers will become more powerful and scalable. This will open up new opportunities for the use of quantum computing in a range of industries.

Quantum computing has the potential to revolutionize various fields, including chemistry and materials science, by solving complex problems that classical computers cannot solve in a reasonable amount of time. With the rapid advancements in the technology of quantum computing, the day is not far when it will be used in various industries.

One area where quantum computing is already being explored is in drug discovery. Traditional drug discovery involves testing millions of compounds to identify potential drug candidates. This is an incredibly time-consuming and expensive process that can take years to complete. However, quantum computers can simulate the behavior of molecules and predict their properties, making it possible to identify potential drug candidates much more quickly and accurately.

Quantum computing can also be used in materials science to discover new materials with desirable properties. For example, by simulating the behavior of atoms and molecules, researchers can discover new materials that are stronger, lighter, and more durable than those currently in use. This can lead to the development of new products and technologies that are more efficient and sustainable.

Another potential application of quantum computing is in the development of new batteries for electric vehicles. By simulating the behavior of atoms and molecules, researchers can design new materials for battery components that are more efficient and longer-lasting than those currently in use. This can help to reduce the cost of electric vehicles and make them more practical for everyday use.

Despite these promising applications, there are still many technological and logistical challenges that need to be overcome before quantum computing can be widely used in chemistry and materials science. For example, the development of fault-tolerant quantum computers capable of performing complex simulations will require advances in hardware and software. Additionally, there is a need for quantum algorithms that are specifically tailored to solve problems in chemistry and materials science.

Quantum computing is still in its early stages and much research needs to be done before it can be utilized to its full potential. One major challenge is the issue of noise and decoherence. Quantum computers are very sensitive to the environment and even a tiny fluctuation can lead to a breakdown in the delicate quantum state, resulting in errors. To overcome this, researchers have proposed a variety of error-correction schemes such as quantum error correction codes, which allow for the detection and correction of errors in a quantum computation.

Another challenge is scaling quantum computers to handle larger and more complex problems. Currently, quantum computers have a limited number of qubits, which limits their computational power. However, researchers are working on developing quantum systems with more qubits and improving the coherence of the qubits to enhance the efficiency and accuracy of the calculations.

The integration of quantum computing into chemistry and materials science has the potential to revolutionize these fields by allowing for the simulation of complex molecular and atomic systems. This could lead to the discovery of new materials with unique properties and the development of new drugs and treatments for diseases.

Quantum computing can also be used to optimize chemical reactions, reducing the time and cost associated with drug development. The ability to simulate chemical reactions at the molecular level could also lead to the development of new materials for energy storage and conversion.

In the field of materials science, quantum computing can help to design and optimize new materials with unique properties. For example, it can be used to predict the electronic and magnetic properties of materials, which can lead to the development of new materials for use in electronic devices.

One potential application of quantum computing in materials science is the development of room-temperature superconductors, which can revolutionize energy distribution and storage. Currently, superconductors must be cooled to very low temperatures to work, making them expensive and impractical for widespread use. However, with the power of quantum computing, researchers could simulate the behavior of electrons in materials, which could lead to the development of room-temperature superconductors.

One potential avenue for harnessing the power of quantum computing in the field of chemistry is through the simulation of molecular systems. Conventional computers struggle to accurately simulate molecular interactions due to the large number of variables involved, and the complex, interconnected relationships between them. However, quantum computers can potentially simulate these interactions much more efficiently, paving the way for the development of new drugs and materials.

One example of the application of quantum computing in this area is the simulation of molecular systems involved in nitrogen fixation. Nitrogen fixation is the process by which nitrogen gas from the atmosphere is converted into a form that can be used by plants and animals. This process is crucial for the growth of crops, and is currently accomplished through the use of industrial fertilizers, which have a significant environmental impact.

A team of researchers at IBM recently used a quantum computer to simulate the nitrogenase enzyme, which is responsible for nitrogen fixation. The simulation accurately predicted the behavior of the enzyme, and provided insights into its mechanism that were not previously possible with conventional computing methods.

Another area of chemistry where quantum computing shows promise is in the design of new materials. Conventional computers are limited in their ability to predict the properties of complex materials, as the interactions between atoms and molecules can be highly nonlinear and difficult to model. However, with quantum computing, it is possible to simulate the behavior of complex materials with much greater accuracy, allowing for the design of new materials with specific properties.

One example of this is the development of new materials for use in solar panels. Solar panels are currently limited in their efficiency due to the materials used in their construction. However, with the help of quantum computing, researchers can simulate the behavior of different materials and identify those with the greatest potential for converting sunlight into electricity.

In addition to its potential applications in chemistry and materials science, quantum computing also has the potential to revolutionize other fields, such as cryptography and machine learning. The ability of quantum computers to factor large numbers quickly could render current encryption methods obsolete, while the ability to process large amounts of data quickly could lead to significant advances in the field of artificial intelligence.

Despite its promise, however, there are still significant challenges to be overcome before quantum computing can reach its full potential. One major challenge is the development of reliable quantum hardware. Quantum computers are highly sensitive to environmental disturbances, and even small disruptions can cause errors in calculations. As a result, researchers are still working to develop ways to control and stabilize the hardware.

Another challenge is the development of quantum algorithms that can take advantage of the unique properties of quantum computing. While there have been some breakthroughs in this area, there is still much work to be done to optimize these algorithms for real-world applications.

In conclusion, quantum computing represents a significant leap in computing technology and has the potential to revolutionize many fields, including chemistry and materials science. By harnessing the power of quantum mechanics, quantum computers can perform complex calculations that are beyond the capability of classical computers, enabling us to tackle problems that were previously unsolvable.

In the field of chemistry, quantum computing can aid in the discovery of new materials and drugs, as well as in the design of more efficient and environmentally friendly chemical processes. The ability of quantum computers to simulate quantum systems in real-time can help researchers understand the behavior of molecules and chemical reactions, which is crucial for the design of new materials and drugs. In addition, quantum computing can aid in the optimization of chemical processes, which can lead to significant energy and cost savings.

In materials science, quantum computing can help in the design of new materials with specific properties, such as high strength and conductivity. The use of quantum computing to simulate the behavior of electrons in materials can aid in the design of materials with novel properties that are currently beyond our understanding. Furthermore, quantum computing can help in the optimization of manufacturing processes, which can lead to more efficient production of materials and devices.

However, there are still significant challenges that must be overcome to realize the full potential of quantum computing. One of the main challenges is the issue of error correction, as quantum computers are highly susceptible to errors due to decoherence and noise. Significant progress has been made in the field of quantum error correction, but there is still a long way to go before error-corrected quantum computers can be realized.

Another challenge is the issue of scalability, as current quantum computers have a limited number of qubits and are not yet capable of solving complex problems. Significant progress has been made in the development of more powerful quantum computers, but it is still unclear whether it is possible to build a fault-tolerant, scalable quantum computer that can solve practical problems.

In summary, quantum computing has the potential to revolutionize the field of chemistry and materials science by enabling the simulation of quantum systems in real-time and the optimization of chemical and manufacturing processes. However, significant challenges must be overcome to realize the full potential of quantum computing, including the issue of error correction and scalability. Nevertheless, the field of quantum computing is rapidly advancing, and it is an exciting time for researchers and engineers working in this field.

CHAPTER VIII

How do our microbiomes interact with our immune systems, and what implications does this have for disease prevention and treatment?

Introduction:

The human body is home to trillions of microorganisms, collectively known as the microbiome, which play important roles in various physiological processes, including digestion, metabolism, and immune function. The microbiome also plays a critical role in regulating immune responses and protecting the body against pathogens. This paper will explore how the microbiome interacts with the immune system and the implications that these interactions have for disease prevention and treatment.

The Microbiome and Immune System:

The microbiome interacts with the immune system through a variety of mechanisms, including direct interactions between microorganisms and immune cells, and the modulation of immune responses by microbiome-derived metabolites.

One of the primary ways that the microbiome interacts with the immune system is through the production of metabolites, such as short-chain fatty acids (SCFAs) and lipopolysaccharides (LPSs). These metabolites can activate or suppress immune responses, depending on the context and the type of metabolite produced. For example, SCFAs have been shown to have anti-inflammatory effects and can promote the production of regulatory T cells, which help to suppress immune responses and prevent autoimmunity. LPSs, on the other hand, can trigger inflammation and activate immune responses.

Another important mechanism by which the microbiome interacts with the immune system is through the direct interaction between microorganisms and immune cells. Certain microorganisms, such as Lactobacillus and Bifidobacterium, have been shown to have immunomodulatory effects and can stimulate the production of cytokines and chemokines that help to regulate immune responses.

Implications for Disease Prevention and Treatment:

The interaction between the microbiome and the immune system has important implications for disease prevention and treatment. Dysbiosis, or an imbalance in the composition of the microbiome, has been linked to a variety of diseases, including inflammatory bowel disease, allergies, and autoimmune diseases.

Recent studies have also shown that the microbiome plays an important role in the response to cancer immunotherapy. Some studies have shown that patients with a more diverse microbiome are more likely to respond to immunotherapy, and that certain bacteria, such as Akkermansia muciniphila and Faecalibacterium prausnitzii, are associated with improved response rates.

Additionally, the microbiome has been shown to play a role in the development of infectious diseases, such as Clostridium difficile infection. Certain probiotics and fecal microbiota transplantation have been used to treat this condition by restoring the microbiome to a healthy state.

Role of Microbiome in Immune System Development:

The microbiome plays a critical role in the development of the immune system, particularly in early life. The establishment of a diverse and stable microbiome in infancy is important for the development of a healthy immune system. Infants acquire their microbiome through exposure to microorganisms in the birth canal, breast milk, and the environment. Disruptions to this process, such as through cesarean section delivery, formula feeding, or antibiotic use, have been linked to an increased risk of immune-related disorders later in life.

The microbiome can also influence immune system function in adulthood. For example, studies have shown that the microbiome plays a role in the maintenance of gut-associated lymphoid tissue (GALT), which is a critical component of the immune system in the gut. Dysbiosis of the gut microbiome has been linked to the development of inflammatory bowel disease, which is characterized by chronic inflammation of the gastrointestinal tract.

Microbiome and Autoimmunity:

Autoimmune diseases occur when the immune system mistakenly attacks healthy cells and tissues in the body. The microbiome has been implicated in the development of autoimmune diseases, as dysbiosis of the microbiome has been linked to an increased risk of autoimmunity.

One mechanism by which dysbiosis of the microbiome can contribute to autoimmunity is through the production of molecular mimicry. Molecular mimicry occurs when microbial antigens are structurally similar to self-antigens, leading to an immune response against both the microbe and self-tissues. This can result in the development of autoimmune diseases such as multiple sclerosis, rheumatoid arthritis, and lupus.

Microbiome and Allergies:

Allergies occur when the immune system overreacts to harmless substances, such as pollen or certain foods. The microbiome has been shown to play a role in the development of allergies, as disruptions to the microbiome can lead to an increased risk of allergy.

One mechanism by which the microbiome can influence allergy risk is through the production of metabolites such as SCFAs, which have been shown to have anti-inflammatory effects and promote the development of regulatory T cells, which help to suppress immune responses and prevent allergy.

Microbiome and Mental Health:

There is growing evidence to suggest that the microbiome plays a role in mental health. Dysbiosis of the gut microbiome has been linked to the development of anxiety, depression, and other mental health disorders. This may be due to the production of microbiome-derived metabolites that can influence neurotransmitter production and brain function.

Additionally, the microbiome-gut-brain axis, which is the bidirectional communication between the gut microbiome and the central nervous system, has been shown to play a role in stress and anxiety responses. This axis may provide a novel target for the development of therapies for mental health disorders.

Microbiome and Cancer:

Emerging evidence suggests that the microbiome may also play a role in cancer development and treatment. Dysbiosis of the gut microbiome has been associated with an increased risk of certain types of cancer, such as colorectal cancer. This may be due to the production of carcinogenic metabolites or the disruption of immune system function.

However, the microbiome may also have a role in cancer treatment. For example, recent studies have shown that the gut microbiome can influence the response to cancer immunotherapy. This is thought to be due to the ability of certain bacteria to stimulate an immune response that can help to fight cancer cells.

Microbiome and Disease Prevention:

Given the important role of the microbiome in immune system function, there is growing interest in the potential for microbiome-based interventions for disease prevention. For example, probiotics, which are live microorganisms that confer health benefits when consumed, have been shown to have immune-modulating effects and may have potential for the prevention and treatment of various diseases.

Additionally, fecal microbiota transplantation (FMT), which involves the transfer of fecal matter from a healthy donor to a recipient, has shown promise for the treatment of certain diseases, particularly those associated with dysbiosis of the gut microbiome.

However, there are still many unknowns when it comes to the use of microbiome-based interventions for disease prevention and treatment. Further research is needed to fully understand the complex interactions between the microbiome and the immune system, as well as to identify the most effective interventions for specific diseases.

Microbiome and Autoimmune Disease:

Autoimmune diseases, such as rheumatoid arthritis, lupus, and multiple sclerosis, are characterized by an overactive immune response that attacks the body's own tissues. Recent research has shown that the microbiome may play a role in the development and progression of autoimmune diseases.

Studies have found that dysbiosis of the gut microbiome can lead to the production of autoantibodies, which are antibodies that attack the body's own tissues. This may be due to the ability of certain bacteria to stimulate the immune system in a way that triggers an autoimmune response.

Additionally, the microbiome may play a role in the regulation of T cells, which are a type of immune cell that help to control the immune response. Dysbiosis of the microbiome can lead to a breakdown in this regulatory function, which can contribute to the development of autoimmune diseases.

Microbiome and Neurological Disorders:

Recent research has also uncovered a link between the microbiome and neurological disorders, such as Alzheimer's disease, Parkinson's disease, and depression. The gut-brain axis, which refers to the bidirectional communication between the gut microbiome and the brain, has been implicated in the development and progression of these disorders.

Studies have found that dysbiosis of the gut microbiome can lead to inflammation and oxidative stress, which are known to contribute to the development of neurological disorders. Additionally, the microbiome may play a role in the production of neurotransmitters, such as serotonin and dopamine, which are important for mood regulation.

Microbiome and Maternal Health:

Finally, the microbiome also plays an important role in maternal health and fetal development. Dysbiosis of the maternal microbiome during pregnancy has been linked to an increased risk of preterm birth, low birth weight, and other pregnancy complications.

Additionally, the composition of the microbiome may influence the development of the fetal immune system, which can have long-term implications for the child's health. Further research is needed to fully understand the role of the microbiome in maternal and fetal health, as well as to identify potential interventions for the prevention of pregnancy complications.

Potential Implications for Disease Prevention and Treatment:

The interactions between the microbiome and the immune system have important implications for disease prevention and treatment. One potential avenue for prevention and treatment is the use of probiotics, which are live microorganisms that confer health benefits when consumed. Probiotics have been shown to improve gut microbiome diversity and promote the growth of beneficial bacteria, which can have a positive impact on immune system function.

Prebiotics, which are non-digestible food components that promote the growth of beneficial bacteria in the gut, may also have potential for disease prevention and treatment. By promoting the growth of beneficial bacteria, prebiotics can improve gut microbiome diversity and stimulate the production of short-chain fatty acids, which have anti-inflammatory properties.

Another potential avenue for disease prevention and treatment is fecal microbiota transplantation (FMT), which involves the transfer of fecal material from a healthy donor into the gut of a patient with a dysbiotic microbiome. FMT has been shown to be effective in treating certain types of infections and inflammatory bowel disease, but further research is needed to fully understand its potential for other conditions.

Additionally, the use of antibiotics, which can have a negative impact on the gut microbiome, may need to be reconsidered in light of the growing understanding of the importance of a healthy microbiome for immune system function. Antibiotic overuse can lead to dysbiosis of the gut microbiome, which can have negative effects on immune system function and increase the risk of various diseases.

Limitations and Future Directions:

While there is growing evidence supporting the role of the microbiome in immune system function, there are still many unanswered questions and limitations to current research. One limitation is the lack of standardization in microbiome research, including variations in sampling methods and analytical techniques. This can make it difficult to compare results across studies and draw definitive conclusions.

Another limitation is the difficulty in determining causality in the relationship between the microbiome and immune system function. While studies have shown correlations between microbiome composition and immune system function, it is unclear whether changes in the microbiome are the cause or the result of changes in immune system function.

Future research directions in this area may include exploring the role of specific bacterial species or strains in immune system function, as well as investigating the impact of environmental factors such as diet and lifestyle on the microbiome-immune system axis. The development of standardized protocols for microbiome research and data analysis will also be important in order to improve the quality and comparability of studies.

Another promising area of research is the development of microbiome-based therapies for disease prevention and treatment. This could include the use of targeted probiotics or prebiotics to modulate the microbiome, as well as the development of microbial-based therapeutics such as bacteriophages or engineered bacteria to treat specific conditions.

Current Challenges in Microbiome Research:

Despite the progress made in microbiome research, there are still many challenges and limitations to be addressed. One major challenge is the lack of standardization in study design, particularly with regard to sampling and analysis protocols. The composition of the microbiome can vary depending on factors such as the site of sampling, the collection method, and the sequencing technology used. This variability can make it difficult to compare results across studies and to draw meaningful conclusions about the role of the microbiome in human health and disease.

Another challenge is the complexity of the microbial communities that make up the human microbiome. These communities are incredibly diverse and can include hundreds of different bacterial, viral, and fungal species, each of which may interact with each other and with the host in unique and complex ways. Understanding these interactions and their impact on human health is a major research goal, but it is also a daunting task that requires significant resources and expertise.

In addition to these technical and scientific challenges, there are also social and ethical considerations to be addressed in microbiome research. For example, there is a need to ensure that research participants are fully informed about the potential risks and benefits of participating in microbiome studies, and that their privacy and autonomy are respected. There is also a need to address issues of equity and access, to ensure that microbiome research benefits all members of society, regardless of their race, gender, or socioeconomic status.

Looking to the Future of Microbiome Research:

Despite the challenges and limitations of current microbiome research, there are many promising avenues for future exploration. One promising direction is the development of microbiome-based interventions for the prevention and treatment of disease. This could include the use of probiotics, prebiotics, or other microbial-based therapies to modulate the microbiome and promote human health.

Another promising direction is the development of new technologies and tools for studying the microbiome. For example, advances in sequencing and computational biology are enabling researchers to generate more detailed and comprehensive data on the microbiome, while new imaging techniques are allowing for the visualization of microbial communities in vivo.

Ultimately, the future of microbiome research will depend on continued investment in both basic and applied research, as well as collaboration across a range of disciplines, including microbiology, immunology, genetics, and bioinformatics. With these efforts, we can hope to gain a more complete understanding of the complex and dynamic interactions between the human microbiome and our health and well-being.

Implications for Disease Prevention and Treatment:

The study of the microbiome has important implications for disease prevention and treatment. Understanding the interactions between the microbiome and the immune system can provide insight into the mechanisms underlying a range of diseases, including inflammatory bowel disease, obesity, and autoimmune disorders. This knowledge can lead to the development of new treatments that target the microbiome, either directly or indirectly through the immune system.

One promising area of research is the use of fecal microbiota transplantation (FMT) to treat a range of conditions, including Clostridium difficile infection, inflammatory bowel disease, and irritable bowel syndrome. FMT involves transferring fecal matter from a healthy donor to a recipient in order to restore a healthy microbiome. This approach has shown promising results in some studies, but more research is needed to determine its safety and effectiveness for different conditions.

Another area of interest is the development of microbial-based therapies, such as probiotics, prebiotics, and synbiotics. Probiotics are live microorganisms that are intended to confer health benefits to the host, while prebiotics are non-digestible dietary fibers that promote the growth of beneficial bacteria. Synbiotics combine both probiotics and prebiotics to enhance their effects. These therapies have been studied for a range of conditions, including diarrhea, constipation, and inflammatory bowel disease, with mixed results. However, advances in our understanding of the microbiome may lead to more targeted and effective use of these therapies in the future.

Understanding the interactions between the microbiome and the immune system may also lead to new approaches for disease prevention. For example, a better understanding of the mechanisms underlying the development of food allergies may lead to the development of interventions that prevent their development. Similarly, knowledge of the interactions between the microbiome and the immune system may lead to the development of vaccines that are tailored to an individual's microbiome.

Challenges and Limitations:

While the study of the microbiome has great potential for disease prevention and treatment, there are also many challenges and limitations that must be addressed. One major challenge is the complexity of the microbiome, which is made up of hundreds of different species and varies widely between individuals. This complexity makes it difficult to identify the specific bacteria or mechanisms that are involved in disease development or prevention.

Another challenge is the difficulty in establishing causality in microbiome research. While there is often a correlation between changes in the microbiome and disease development, it can be difficult to determine whether these changes are a cause or a result of the disease. Additionally, many factors can influence the microbiome, including diet, medications, and other environmental factors, which makes it difficult to isolate the effects of the microbiome from other factors.

There are also limitations in the tools and technologies available for studying the microbiome. While advances in sequencing technologies have greatly expanded our ability to identify and characterize the bacteria in the microbiome, there are still limitations in our ability to measure the functional activity of the microbiome, particularly in complex microbial communities.

Finally, there are ethical and safety considerations associated with microbiome research, particularly with regards to the use of FMT and other microbial-based therapies. While these therapies have shown promise in some studies, there are still many unknowns about their long-term safety and efficacy. Additionally, there are concerns about the potential transfer of pathogens or antibiotic resistance genes through FMT.

Applications and Future Directions:

Despite the challenges and limitations, there are already a number of practical applications of microbiome research for disease prevention and treatment. One promising area of research is the use of probiotics and other microbial-based therapies to modulate the microbiome and improve immune function. For example, probiotics have been shown to improve outcomes in patients with inflammatory bowel disease, and other microbial-based therapies are being explored for a range of conditions, including allergies, obesity, and cancer.

Another promising application of microbiome research is in the development of personalized medicine approaches. By analyzing an individual's microbiome, it may be possible to identify specific microbial signatures that are associated with disease risk or treatment response. This information could then be used to develop personalized interventions to optimize health and prevent disease.

Looking forward, there are a number of important areas for future research in the field of microbiome-immune interactions. One key area of focus will be the development of more precise and sensitive tools for studying the microbiome and its interactions with the immune system. This will require continued investment in both sequencing technologies and functional assays that allow us to measure the activity of the microbiome in vivo.

Another important area of future research will be the development of more targeted and effective microbial-based therapies. While FMT and other therapies have shown promise in some studies, there is still much we do not know about the long-term safety and efficacy of these treatments. Further research is needed to better understand the mechanisms of action of these therapies and to develop more targeted and effective interventions.

It will be important to better understand the role of the microbiome in different disease states and to identify specific microbial signatures that are associated with disease risk or treatment response. This information will be critical for the development of personalized medicine approaches and for the identification of new targets for drug development.

While there is much excitement about the potential of the microbiome-immune system interaction, there are also a number of challenges and limitations that must be addressed. One major challenge is the high degree of interpersonal variability in the composition and function of the microbiome. While there are some general patterns in the microbial communities of healthy individuals, there is also significant individual variability, and this can make it difficult to draw firm conclusions about the role of the microbiome in health and disease.

Another challenge is the lack of standardization in microbiome research methods. There are many different methods for analyzing the microbiome, and the choice of method can have a significant impact on the results. This makes it difficult to compare results across studies and to draw firm conclusions about the microbiome's role in health and disease.

In addition to these challenges, there are also a number of limitations to current microbiome research methods. For example, many studies are limited by small sample sizes, which can make it difficult to draw statistically significant conclusions. There is also a lack of longitudinal studies that follow individuals over time, which makes it difficult to understand how the microbiome changes over the course of a lifetime and how these changes relate to health outcomes.

Another limitation is the difficulty of studying the microbiome in vivo. While there are many techniques for analyzing the microbiome in vitro, it is much more difficult to study the microbiome in the context of a living organism. This makes it challenging to understand the complex interactions between the microbiome and the immune system and to develop targeted interventions.

Implications for Disease Prevention and Treatment:

While much research is still needed to fully understand the microbiome-immune system interaction, there are already some promising implications for disease prevention and treatment. Here are some examples:

Infection Prevention: The microbiome plays an important role in protecting the body from pathogens, and research has shown that alterations in the microbiome can increase the risk of infection. By understanding how the microbiome protects against infection, researchers may be able to develop new strategies for preventing and treating infections.

Chronic Diseases: The microbiome has been implicated in a wide range of chronic diseases, including inflammatory bowel disease, diabetes, and obesity. By studying the microbiome in the context of these diseases, researchers may be able to identify new targets for treatment and develop more effective therapies.

Cancer Treatment: Recent research has suggested that the microbiome may play a role in the response to cancer treatments such as immunotherapy. By understanding how the microbiome affects the immune system's response to cancer, researchers may be able to develop new strategies for improving the efficacy of cancer treatments.

Fecal Microbiota Transplantation (FMT): FMT is an experimental therapy that involves transplanting fecal material from a healthy donor into the gut of a recipient with a microbiome-related disease. While more research is needed to fully understand the long-term safety and efficacy of this approach, early studies have shown promise for the treatment of conditions such as Clostridium difficile infection and inflammatory bowel disease.

Personalized Medicine: The high degree of interpersonal variability in the composition and function of the microbiome suggests that a personalized approach to medicine may be needed in order to fully harness the potential of the microbiome. By understanding how individual microbiomes affect health and disease, researchers may be able to develop personalized treatment strategies that are tailored to the needs of individual patients.

Limitations and Future Directions:

While the research into the microbiome-immune system interaction has made significant strides in recent years, there are still many limitations and areas for future investigation. Some of the limitations of current research include:

Sample Size and Diversity: Many studies of the microbiome have small sample sizes or include only a limited range of participants. As a result, it can be difficult to generalize findings to larger populations, or to understand the full range of diversity in the human microbiome.

Causality: While many studies have found associations between the microbiome and immune system function, it can be difficult to establish causality. In other words, it can be challenging to determine whether changes in the microbiome are directly responsible for changes in immune system function, or if other factors are at play.

Data Analysis and Interpretation: The vast amount of data generated by microbiome research can be challenging to analyze and interpret, and there is still a need for more standardized methods for analyzing and reporting results.

Lack of Intervention Studies: While there have been some studies examining the effects of interventions such as probiotics or prebiotics on the microbiome and immune system, more research is needed in this area to fully understand the potential therapeutic benefits of these approaches.

Future directions for research in the microbiome-immune system interaction may include:

Longitudinal Studies: Long-term studies of the microbiome and immune system could help researchers to better understand the dynamics of this complex interaction over time.

Mechanistic Studies: Further mechanistic studies could help to establish causal relationships between the microbiome and immune system, and to identify specific pathways or mechanisms that are involved in this interaction.

Intervention Studies: Large-scale intervention studies could help to determine the efficacy and safety of treatments such as FMT or probiotics for a range of conditions.

Personalized Medicine: The high degree of variability in the microbiome suggests that personalized medicine may be necessary to fully leverage the potential of the microbiome-immune system interaction. Future research could focus on developing personalized treatment strategies that take into account individual microbiome profiles.

Disease Implications:

The relationship between the microbiome and the immune system has important implications for a range of diseases and conditions. Some examples include:

Inflammatory Bowel Disease (IBD): IBD is a group of chronic inflammatory conditions that affect the digestive tract. It has been found that individuals with IBD have an altered gut microbiome, and that this may contribute to the development and progression of the disease.

Allergies: Allergies are characterized by an exaggerated immune response to harmless substances, such as pollen or dust. Recent research has suggested that alterations in the microbiome may contribute to the development of allergies, by influencing the development and function of the immune system.

Autoimmune Diseases: Autoimmune diseases occur when the immune system attacks healthy cells and tissues in the body. Some evidence suggests that alterations in the microbiome may contribute to the development of autoimmune diseases, by triggering an immune response against host tissues.

Cancer: There is some evidence to suggest that alterations in the microbiome may contribute to the development and progression of cancer, by influencing immune system function and the development of the tumor microenvironment.

Infectious Diseases: The microbiome plays a critical role in protecting against infectious diseases, by competing with pathogenic bacteria for resources and by promoting the development of a healthy immune system. Some research suggests that alterations in the microbiome may increase the risk of certain infectious diseases, such as Clostridioides difficile infection.

Implications for Treatment and Prevention:

The relationship between the microbiome and immune system also has important implications for the development of new treatments and prevention strategies. Some potential approaches include:

Probiotics: Probiotics are live microorganisms that are intended to have health benefits when consumed. They may work by promoting the growth of beneficial bacteria in the gut, or by directly interacting with the immune system.

Prebiotics: Prebiotics are non-digestible fibers that are intended to promote the growth of beneficial bacteria in the gut. They may work by providing a food source for beneficial bacteria, or by promoting changes in the gut environment that are favorable to these bacteria.

Fecal Microbiota Transplantation (FMT): FMT involves the transfer of fecal material from a healthy donor to a recipient, with the aim of restoring a healthy microbiome. This approach has been shown to be effective in treating recurrent Clostridioides difficile infection, and is being explored as a potential treatment for other conditions.

Diet: Diet is a key factor in shaping the composition of the microbiome, and may be an important factor in disease prevention and treatment. A diet that is high in fiber and plant-based foods has been associated with a more diverse and beneficial microbiome.

Antibiotics: While antibiotics can be life-saving in the treatment of bacterial infections, they also have the potential to disrupt the microbiome and contribute to the development of antibiotic-resistant bacteria. Efforts to develop new antibiotics that are more targeted and have fewer side effects on the microbiome are ongoing.

The interaction between the microbiome and the immune system is complex and multifaceted. However, as research in this area continues to grow, we are beginning to gain a better understanding of the ways in which these two systems work together and impact our health. By understanding the relationship between the microbiome and the immune system, we may be able to develop new strategies for disease prevention and treatment that could have a significant impact on public health.

One potential implication of this research is the development of new probiotic treatments that are designed to target specific diseases or health conditions. For example, probiotics may be used to help prevent or treat conditions such as inflammatory bowel disease, autoimmune disorders, and allergies by modulating the immune response. By understanding the specific interactions between the microbiome and the immune system in these conditions, researchers may be able to develop more targeted and effective probiotic therapies.

Another potential area of application is the development of personalized medicine approaches that take into account an individual's unique microbiome profile. By understanding the specific ways in which an individual's microbiome interacts with their immune system, doctors may be able to identify which treatments or interventions are most likely to be effective for that person. This could lead to more personalized and effective treatments for a wide range of conditions.

Research into the microbiome and the immune system has also shed light on the potential role of these systems in mental health. Recent studies have suggested that imbalances in the microbiome may be associated with a range of mental health conditions, including depression and anxiety. This is thought to be due, at least in part, to the impact of the microbiome on the immune system and the subsequent effects on inflammation and neurotransmitter production.

There is also evidence to suggest that interventions that target the microbiome and immune system may have a beneficial effect on mental health. For example, probiotics have been shown to improve symptoms of depression and anxiety in some studies. Additionally, treatments that target the immune system, such as anti-inflammatory medications, may also have a beneficial effect on mental health.

Finally, the interaction between the microbiome and the immune system has important implications for public health and disease prevention. By understanding the factors that impact the microbiome and the immune system, we may be able to identify strategies for preventing a range of diseases and conditions. For example, maintaining a healthy diet, exercising regularly, and avoiding exposure to certain environmental toxins may all have a positive impact on the microbiome and the immune system.

In conclusion, the microbiome and immune system are closely intertwined and have important implications for disease prevention and treatment. The microbiome plays a critical role in modulating the immune system and regulating inflammation, and imbalances in the microbiome can contribute to a range of health conditions. By understanding the complex interplay between these systems, we can develop new strategies for disease prevention and treatment that take into account the importance of the microbiome in overall health. As research in this area continues to evolve, we are likely to gain a better understanding of the specific mechanisms underlying these interactions and to develop more targeted interventions that can improve health outcomes for individuals and populations. Ultimately, a greater understanding of the microbiome-immune system axis has the potential to revolutionize our approach to disease prevention and treatment, leading to improved health outcomes and better quality of life for people around the world.